Jack C. Richards & Chuck Sandy

Passages
Third Edition

Student's Book **1B**

CAMBRIDGE UNIVERSITY PRESS

CAMBRIDGE
UNIVERSITY PRESS

University Printing House, Cambridge CB2 8BS, United Kingdom

One Liberty Plaza, 20th Floor, New York, NY 10006, USA

477 Williamstown Road, Port Melbourne, VIC 3207, Australia

314–321, 3rd Floor, Plot 3, Splendor Forum, Jasola District Centre, New Delhi – 110025, India

79 Anson Road, #06–04/06, Singapore 079906

Cambridge University Press is part of the University of Cambridge.

It furthers the University's mission by disseminating knowledge in the pursuit of education, learning and research at the highest international levels of excellence.

www.cambridge.org
Information on this title: www.cambridge.org/9781107627062

© Cambridge University Press 2015

This publication is in copyright. Subject to statutory exception and to the provisions of relevant collective licensing agreements, no reproduction of any part may take place without the written permission of Cambridge University Press.

First published 1998
Second edition 2008
Reprinted 2018

Printed in Italy by Rotolito S.p.A.

A catalogue record for this publication is available from the British Library

ISBN 978-1-107-62705-5 Student's Book 1
ISBN 978-1-107-62701-7 Student's Book 1A
ISBN 978-1-107-62706-2 Student's Book 1B
ISBN 978-1-107-62725-3 Workbook 1
ISBN 978-1-107-62718-5 Workbook 1A
ISBN 978-1-107-62720-8 Workbook 1B
ISBN 978-1-107-62768-0 Teacher's Edition 1 with Assessment Audio CD/CD-ROM
ISBN 978-1-107-62754-3 Class Audio 1 CDs
ISBN 978-1-107-62769-7 Full Contact 1
ISBN 978-1-107-62771-0 Full Contact 1A
ISBN 978-1-107-62772-7 Full Contact 1B
ISBN 978-1-107-62762-8 DVD 1
ISBN 978-1-107-66626-9 Presentation Plus 1

Additional resources for this publication at www.cambridge.org/passages

Cambridge University Press has no responsibility for the persistence or accuracy of URLs for external or third-party internet websites referred to in this publication, and does not guarantee that any content on such websites is, or will remain, accurate or appropriate. Information regarding prices, travel timetables, and other factual information given in this work is correct at the time of first printing but Cambridge University Press does not guarantee the accuracy of such information thereafter.

Art direction, book design, layout services, and photo research: Q2A / Bill Smith
Audio production: John Marshall Media
Video production: Steadman Productions

Authors' Acknowledgments

A great number of people contributed to the development of *Passages Third Edition*. Particular thanks are owed to the following reviewers and institutions, as their insights and suggestions have helped define the content and format of the third edition:

Paulo A. Machado, Rio de Janeiro, Brazil; Simone C. Wanguestel, Niterói, Brazil; Athiná Arcadinos Leite, **ACBEU**, Salvador, Brazil; Lauren Osowski, **Adult Learning Center**, Nashua, NH, USA; Brenda Victoria, **AIF System**, Santiago, Dominican Republic; Alicia Mitchell-Boncquet, **ALPS Language School**, Seattle, WA, USA; Scott C. Welsh, **Arizona State University**, Tempe, AZ, USA; Silvia Corrêa, **Associação Alumni**, São Paulo, Brazil; Henrick Oprea, **Atlantic Idiomas**, Brasília, Brazil; Márcia Lima, **B.A. English School**, Goiânia, Brazil; Carlos Andrés Mejía Gómez, **BNC Centro Colombo Americano Pereira**, Pereira, Colombia; Tanja Jakimoska, **Brava Training**, Rio de Janeiro, Brazil; Paulo Henrique Gomes de Abreu, **Britannia International English**, Rio de Janeiro, Brazil; Gema Kuri Rodríguez, **Business & English**, Puebla, Mexico; Isabela Villas Boas, **Casa Thomas Jefferson**, Brasília, Brazil; Inara Lúcia Castillo Couto, **CEL-LEP**, São Paulo, Brazil; Ana Cristina Hebling Meira, **Centro Cultural Brasil-Estados Unidos**, Campinas, Brazil; Juliana Costa da Silva, **Centro de Cultura Anglo Americana**, Rio de Janeiro, Brazil; Heriberto Díaz Vázquez, **Centro de Investigación y Docencia Económicas**, Mexico City, Mexico; D. L. Dorantes-Salas, **Centro de Investigaciones Biológicas del Noroeste**, La Paz, Mexico; Elizabeth Carolina Llatas Castillo, **Centro Peruano Americano El Cultural**, Trujillo-La Libertad, Peru; Márcia M. A. de Brito, **Chance Language Center**, Rio de Janeiro, Brazil; Rosalinda Heredia, **Colegio Motolinia**, San Juan del Río, Mexico; Maria Regina Pereira Filgueiras, **College Language Center**, Londrina, Brazil; Lino Mendoza Rodriguez, **Compummunicate**, Izúcar de Matamoros, Mexico; Maria Lucia Sciamarelli, **Cultura Inglesa**, Campinas, Brazil; Elisabete Thess, **Cultura Inglesa**, Petrópolis, Brazil; Catarina M. B. Pontes Kruppa, **Cultura Inglesa**, São Paulo, Brazil; Sheila Lima, **Curso Oxford**, Rio de Janeiro, Brazil; Elaine Florencio, Beth Vasconcelos, **English House Corporate**, Rio de Janeiro, Brazil; Vasti Rodrigues e Silva, **Fox Idiomas**, Rio de Janeiro, Brazil; Ricardo Ramos Miguel Cézar, Walter Júnior Ribeiro Silva, **Friends Language Center**, Itapaci, Brazil; Márcia Maria Pedrosa Sá Freire de Souza, **IBEU**, Rio de Janeiro, Brazil; Jerusa Rafael, **IBEUV**, Vitória, Brazil; Lilianne de Souza Oliveira, **ICBEU**, Manaus, Brazil; Liviane Santana Paulino de Carvalho, **ICBEU**, São Luís, Brazil; Manuel Marrufo Vásquez, **iempac Instituto de Enseñanza del Idioma Ingles**, Tequila, Mexico; Nora Aquino, **Instituto de Ciencias y Humanidades Tabasco**, Villahermosa, Mexico; Andrea Grimaldo, **Instituto Laurens**, Monterrey, Mexico; Cenk Aykut, Staci Jenkins, Kristen Okada, **Interactive College of Technology**, Chamblee, GA, USA; Imeen Manahan-Vasquez, Zuania Serrano, **Interactive Learning Systems**, Pasadena, TX, USA; Nicholas J. Jackson, **Jackson English School**, Uruapan, Mexico; Marc L. Cummings, **Jefferson Community and Technical College**, Louisville, KY, USA; Solange Nery Veloso, **Nery e Filho Idiomas**, Rio de Janeiro, Brazil; Tomas Sparano Martins, **Phil Young's English School**, Curitiba, Brazil; Paulo Cezar Lira Torres, **PRIME Language Center**, Vitória, Brazil; Angie Vasconcellos, **Robin English School**, Petrópolis, Brazil; Barbara Raifsnider, **San Diego Community College District**, San Diego, CA, USA; James Drury de Matos Fonseca, **SENAC**, Fortaleza, Brazil; Manoel Fialho da Silva Neto, **SENAC**, Recife, Brazil; Marilyn Ponder, **Tecnológico de Monterrey**, Irapuato, Mexico; Linda M. Holden, **The College of Lake County**, Grayslake, IL, USA; Janaína da Silva Cardoso, **UERJ**, Rio de Janeiro, Brazil; Gustavo Reges Ferreira, Sandlei Moraes de Oliveira, **UFES**, Vitória, Brazil; Nancy Alarcón Mendoza, **UNAM, Facultad de Estudios Superiores Zaragoza**, Mexico City, Mexico; Rosa Awilda López Fernández, **UNAPEC**, Santo Domingo, Dominican Republic; Vera Lúcia Ratide, **Unilínguas**, São Leopoldo, Brazil; Elsa Yolanda Cruz Maldonado, **Universidad Autónoma de Chiapas**, Tapachula, Mexico; Deida Perea, **Universidad Autónoma de Ciudad Juárez**, Ciudad Juárez, Mexico; Gabriela Ladrón de Guevara de León, **Universidad Autónoma de la Ciudad de México**, Mexico City, Mexico; Juan Manuel Ardila Prada, **Universidad Autónoma de Occidente**, Cali, Colombia; Lizzete G. Acosta Cruz, **Universidad Autónoma de Zacatecas**, Fresnillo, Mexico; Ary Guel, Fausto Noriega, Areli Martínez Suaste, **Universidad Autónoma de Zacatecas**, Zacatecas, Mexico; Gabriela Cortés Sánchez, **Universidad Autónoma Metropolitana Azcapotzalco**, Mexico City, Mexico; Secundino Isabeles Flores, Guillermo Guadalupe Duran Garcia, Maria Magdalena Cass Zubiria, **Universidad de Colima**, Colima, Mexico; Alejandro Rodríguez Sánchez, **Universidad del Golfo de México Norte**, Orizaba, Mexico; Fabiola Meneses Argüello, **Universidad La Salle Cancún**, Cancún, Mexico; Claudia Isabel Fierro Castillo, **Universidad Politécnica de Chiapas**, Tuxtla Gutierrez, Mexico; Eduardo Aguirre Rodríguez, M.A. Carolina Labastida Villa, **Universidad Politécnica de Quintana Roo**, Cancún, Mexico; Gabriela de Jesús Aubry González, **Universidad TecMilenio Campus Veracruz**, Boca del Rio, Mexico; Frank Ramírez Marín, **Universidad Veracruzana**, Boca del Río, Mexico.

Additional thanks are owed to Alex Tilbury for revising the Self-assessment charts, Paul MacIntyre for revising the Grammar Plus section, and Karen Kawaguchi for writing the Vocabulary Plus section.

Welcome to Passages!

Congratulations! You have learned the basics; now it's time to raise your English to a whole new level.

Your journey through each unit of *Passages Third Edition* will include a range of activities that will **progressively expand your language ability** in a variety of contexts, including formal and informal communication.

Along the way, you will encounter frequent communication reviews and progress checks that will **systematically consolidate your learning**, while **additional grammar and vocabulary practice** is available whenever you need it in the Grammar Plus and Vocabulary Plus sections in the back of this book.

RAISING YOUR ENGLISH TO A WHOLE NEW LEVEL
Unique features to boost your English proficiency!

STARTING POINT presents new grammar in a variety of real-world contexts.

VOCABULARY expands upon prior knowledge and improves vocabulary building skills.
NEW Vocabulary Plus: extra vocabulary practice when you need it!

GRAMMAR is explored in context and builds on previously encountered structures.
Grammar Plus: extra grammar explanations and practice when you need it!

SPEAKING activities spark lively discussions focusing on interesting and relevant situations.

5 LISTENING
Life in Sydney

A Listen to Maria and Ian talk about life in Sydney. Who seems to enjoy living there more?

B Listen again. Which person has these opinions? Choose Maria, Ian, or both.

	Maria	Ian	Both
1. It's easy to get around Sydney.	☐	☐	☐
2. The beaches are great.	☐	☐	☐
3. The rents are expensive.	☐	☐	☐
4. It's a fun place to live.	☐	☐	☐
5. The restaurants are all expensive.	☐	☐	☐
6. Life is better in a smaller town.	☐	☐	☐

LISTENING activities sharpen essential listening comprehension skills.

6 DISCUSSION
Quality of life

A Rate these quality-of-life issues as very important (2), important (1), or not important (0). Can you add one more to the list?

Quality of Life
- ____ affordable housing
- ____ a variety of restaurants
- ____ beautiful parks
- ____ convenient public transportation
- ____ exciting ...
- ____ first-clas...
- ____ historic ...
- ____ low crim...

B **Pair work** Which three issues are the most impor... considering where to live? Explain why.

"I guess affordable housing and exciting nightlife are the m... find a place I could afford that was near someplace fun."
"I know what you mean. But for me, I guess low crime rate... I want to live somewhere where I feel safe. I don't mind if ..."

C **Class activity** Share your answers with your clas... mentioned most often?

24 UNIT 3 Exploring new cities

Passages Third Edition is a two-level course that will open the door to communicating with greater fluency and proficiency, with:

- **more sophisticated** real-world grammar and vocabulary,
- **thought-provoking** discussions and academic writing activities,
- **more challenging** listening and reading comprehension topics.

7 WRITING
Brainstorming

Brainstorming means making a list of ideas about a topic. Then you can use this list to come up with a topic sentence and ideas to support it.

A **Group work** Brainstorm as many ideas as you can to add to the dos and don'ts for living on a budget.

Living on a Tight Bu...

Do	Don't
• compare prices	• buy the f...
• look for sales	• buy bran...
• check ads for used items	• use cred...

B **Group work** Brainstorm dos and don'ts for one of ...
- getting over a bad cold
- staying safe in a b...

C Read this paragraph about living on a tight budget. ... sentence and a similar paragraph about your topic u...

Living on a tight budget is easy if you follow som... shopping. First of all, you should never buy somethi... need to check at least a few other stores and go on... don't be in a hurry! If you take your time, you might ... now, ask a salesperson if there's going to be one so... secondhand, items. You can check in the newspape... for. Finally, you might get a better price at some sto... credit card, so be sure to ask about cash discounts.

D **Pair work** Exchange brainstorming lists and parag... Then answer the questions.
1. How many brainstorming ideas did your partner u... chose the best ones?
2. Do you have any questions about your partner's p... you disagree with?
3. Can you think of a good title for your partner's pa...

WRITING tasks build academic writing skills through step-by-step activities.

7 READING
Cyber-begging

A **Pair work** Imagine that a stranger asked you for money to help pay off a frivolous debt. Would you help? Tell your partner. Then read the article.

Can you spare a dime for my Gucci bills?

There was a time when Karyn Bosnak couldn't pay a $59.00 bill at the grocery store. She was officially broke. She didn't have enough money to get on the subway, but she looked rich. She was a television producer, earned $900 a week, and had a closetful of designer labels like Gucci and Louis Vuitton. But she also had a $20,221.40 credit card bill and an empty bank account. Karyn decided that it was time for a change. She built a website and simply asked people to help her out by sending her a buck or two.

On the site, Karyn honestly explained her situation, Gucci shoes and all. "If 20,000 people gave me just $1, I'd be home free, and I'm sure there are 20,000 people out there who can afford to give me $1." Amazingly, it worked. Her website was visited by more than a million people. Although most donors just gave a few dollars, one generous donor sent $1,000. She was on TV and in newspapers and magazines. She was offered a book deal and a movie contract. And of course, she was able to pay off her credit card debt.

She also sold her designer clothes on eBay. In her closet, where the Gucci purses once sat, Karyn keeps all the letters that people have sent her.

She's received teddy bears, subscriptions to *Vogue*, Dunkin' Donuts coupons, backpacks, jewelry, cat food, and candles.

It's hard to understand why so many people helped a total stranger pay off her huge credit card bill. Why did they do it? Karyn explains, "I was just honest about what happened; I didn't make up some sob story about saving the world." Her donors think it's funny and original, she argues, and view it less as a charity than as an entertainment site.

Imitators have sprung up all over the Internet, some with outrageously selfish requests like a BMW or a house. Actually, Karyn was not the first person to put up a website asking strangers for money. The practice has a name: "cyber-begging." Most sites receive little traffic and even less cash.

Karyn also had thousands of enemies and critics. People sent her hate mail and scolded her on websites. Karyn says she never let this anger bother her. "They are probably jealous they didn't think of it," she explains.

Source: "Brother, can you spare a dime for my Gucci bills?" by Janelle Brown, Salon.com

READING passages drawn from authentic sources promote critical thinking and analysis.

B Read the article again and answer the questions. Then compare your answers with a partner.
1. Why was Karyn in financial trouble?
2. What was her main solution to her problem? What else did she do?
3. Why did so many people respond positively to her website?

C **Group work** Discuss these questions. Then share your answers with the class.
1. Do you think Karyn was unethical, or was she simply clever?
2. What would you have done if you were Karyn?

LESSON B Information overload 61

KEEP MOVING UP!
More support is always available – when and where you need it!

| The **WORKBOOK** provides extensive practice of grammar and vocabulary as well as additional reading and writing activities. | The **ONLINE WORKBOOK** – a digital version of the Workbook – enables your teacher to provide instant feedback on your work. | The **PASSAGES ONLINE VOCABULARY ACCELERATOR** increases the speed and ease of learning new vocabulary through powerful and innovative digital learning techniques. |

v

Plan of BOOK 1B

	FUNCTIONS	GRAMMAR	VOCABULARY
UNIT 7 The information age pages 54–61			
A A weird, wired world B Information overload	■ Talking about trends ■ Participating in a debate ■ Giving opinions	■ Passive of present continuous, present perfect, future ■ Negative and tag questions for giving opinions	■ Technology buzzwords ■ Expressions for connecting ideas formally ■ Words for forms of communication
UNIT 8 Putting the mind to work pages 62–69			
A Exploring creativity B Ideas that work	■ Describing job qualifications ■ Offering solutions to problems ■ Commenting on facts ■ Analyzing reasons	■ Reduced relative clauses ■ Non-defining relative clauses as sentence modifiers	■ Qualities of creative people ■ Collocations for problem solving
UNIT 9 Generally speaking pages 70–77			
A How typical are you? B Problems and solutions	■ Comparing customs and habits ■ Presenting contrasting information ■ Making generalizations ■ Talking about past habits	■ Clauses and phrases showing contrast and exception ■ Past habitual with *used to* and *would*	■ Expressions related to accepting or changing things ■ Expressions with *keep* and *stay*
UNITS 7–9 Communication review pages 78–79			
UNIT 10 The art of complaining pages 80–87			
A That really bugs me! B Let's do something about it!	■ Describing everyday annoyances ■ Describing complaining styles ■ Making and responding to complaints ■ Identifying ways to avoid problems ■ Discussing advice	■ Relative clauses and noun clauses ■ Simple and complex indirect questions	■ Expressions with *drive*, *get*, and *make* ■ *-ed* words that describe feelings
UNIT 11 Values pages 88–95			
A How honest are you? B Taking stock	■ Discussing hypothetical situations ■ Talking about values ■ Expressing wishes and regrets	■ Present unreal conditional with *unless*, *only if*, and *even if* ■ Wishes and regrets	■ Forming antonyms with prefixes ■ Adjectives that describe ethics and attitudes ■ Adjectives and nouns referring to personal values
UNIT 12 Moving around pages 96–103			
A Culture shock B Traveler or tourist?	■ Predicting the future ■ Comparing and contrasting customs ■ Making hypotheses ■ Giving advice ■ Describing preferences	■ Future perfect and future perfect continuous ■ Mixed conditionals	■ Expressions ending with prepositions ■ Compound adjectives
UNITS 10–12 Communication review pages 104–105			
GRAMMAR PLUS: Additional grammar practice and explanation pages 118–129			
VOCABULARY PLUS: Additional vocabulary practice pages 136–141			

SPEAKING	LISTENING	WRITING	READING
- Talking about Internet trends - Debating whether social networking is a positive or negative influence - Giving opinions on modern information technology - Discussing potential future technologies	- Three people talk about social networking - A news report describes health problems caused by technology	- Writing a product or service review	- "Can you spare a dime for my Gucci bills?": A woman uses the Internet to get money to pay off a frivolous debt
- Discussing jobs that require creativity - Taking a creativity quiz - Suggesting new uses for everyday items - Talking about creative thinking habits - Choosing the inventions that have had the greatest impact on modern life - Explaining why new products are invented	- Three employees explain how their jobs are creative - Two descriptions of important business and product ideas	- Choosing when to begin a new paragraph - Writing a composition about a creative or unique person	- "The Man Who Taught the World to Sing": A profile of the man who invented karaoke
- Talking about what is typical - Discussing what makes you typical or not - Discussing the effect of major life changes - Giving advice in a role play	- Three people discuss how they're unique or typical - Three people describe how they solved a problem	- Identifying supporting statements - Writing a paragraph with supporting statements	- "Painting and Problem Solving: Four Lessons": How problem solving and the dynamics of painting are alike
- Discussing how to handle irritating situations - Comparing styles of complaining - Role-playing complaints - Describing how difficult situations make you feel - Stating consumer complaints	- Two people describe irritating situations - A man uses an automated phone menu	- Writing a message of complaint	- "Dave Carroll Airs a Complaint": A musician posts music videos to complain about an airline
- Discussing the results of a survey on ethical behavior - Comparing what you would do about different ethical dilemmas - Discussing your experiences with unreliable people or services - Talking about values that are important to you - Explaining what you'd choose if you were given three wishes	- Two people describe being confronted by an ethical dilemma - Three people talk about the values that are most important to them	- Writing a thesis statement - Writing a four-paragraph composition about a happy memory or a regret	- "New York Honors a Hero": How a construction worker became a hero
- Describing the benefits and challenges of living abroad - Comparing customs between Canada and your country - Sharing bad travel experiences - Planning a trip with your group	- Three people talk about their experiences living abroad - Two people describe travel mishaps	- Writing conclusions - Writing a composition about living or traveling abroad	- "Get Yourself Lost": The best way to experience a foreign destination

7 THE INFORMATION AGE
LESSON A ▶ A weird, wired world

1 STARTING POINT
Internet trends

A Look at these Internet trends. Choose the ones that affect you.

Internet Trends

NOW...
- ☐ Music fans have been given access to nearly unlimited music libraries in "the cloud."
- ☐ Increasingly, information about Internet users is being collected for marketing purposes.
- ☐ Many traditional textbooks have been replaced by online versions.
- ☐ With the development of new online tools, more employees are being allowed to work remotely for part of their workweek.

IN THE FUTURE...
- ☐ Most store purchases will be made by using a mobile device linked to an online account. Cash or credit cards will rarely be used.
- ☐ More and more doctor's examinations are likely going to be done over the Internet.
- ☐ More candidates for employment will be identified, interviewed, and hired online.
- ☐ The Internet is going to be subjected to a greater number of hacker attacks due to the increasing amount of personal information stored online.

B Pair work What did people do before these trends appeared?

"People used to buy CDs, and they put them in CD players to listen to them."

2 VOCABULARY
Technology buzzwords

A Match the terms on the left with the definitions on the right.

1. download ____
2. app ____
3. post ____
4. blog ____
5. Wi-Fi ____
6. the cloud ____
7. podcast ____
8. spyware ____
9. text ____
10. virus ____

a. wireless connection to the Internet
b. a radio or TV show downloadable from the Internet
c. transfer files to your computer or smartphone
d. harmful software that attacks computers or phones
e. send a short typed message from a cell phone
f. put something on the Internet for others to see
g. software that secretly records your online activity
h. a program often used on mobile devices
i. large, remote information storage areas on the Internet
j. an online journal or newsletter, usually of personal opinions

B Pair work Which of these technologies do you have experience with? When do you use them? Why?

"I've been downloading music and videos for years. And if I'm too busy to watch TV, I download podcasts of interesting shows to my smartphone. It's great!"

VOCABULARY PLUS see page 136

3 GRAMMAR

Passive of present continuous, present perfect, future

Use the passive for actions where the emphasis is on the object of the action.

Use the passive of the present continuous for ongoing actions.
More employees **are being allowed** to work remotely for part of their workweek.

Use the passive of the present perfect for recently completed actions.
Music fans **have been given** access to nearly unlimited music libraries in "the cloud."

Use *will* + passive or *be going to* + passive for actions that will begin in the future.
Most store purchases **will be made** by using a mobile device linked to an online account.
More and more doctor's examinations are likely **going to be done** over the Internet.

GRAMMAR PLUS see page 118

A Look at the Starting Point on page 54 again. Can you find more examples of each passive?

B Complete the sentences with the correct passive form of the verb in parentheses. Sometimes more than one answer is possible.

1. Thousands of computers already ___have been infected___ (infect) by spyware.
2. Currently, the cloud _____ (utilize) by a large number of businesses.
3. Thousands of blogs _____ (start) on all sorts of topics every day.
4. In coming years, even more fun game apps _____ (develop) for the youth market.
5. Nowadays, teen Internet use _____ (monitor) by concerned parents.
6. These days, podcasts _____ (download) by people of all ages.
7. Many computer viruses _____ (create) by teenagers.
8. In the future, Wi-Fi _____ (make) available in most public places.

4 LISTENING

Social networking: Different opinions

A Listen to three people's opinions about social networking. What do they mainly use it for?

1. _____ 2. _____ 3. _____

B Listen again. Choose the correct answers to complete the sentences.

1. Michael believes that social networking at work . . .
   ☐ a. should be restricted.   ☐ b. makes workers happier.

2. In the case of children, Lisa believes that social networking . . .
   ☐ a. teaches social skills.   ☐ b. is potentially harmful.

3. Daniel is careful about what he uploads or posts so people won't . . .
   ☐ a. steal his work.   ☐ b. form a bad opinion of him.

LESSON A A weird, wired world 55

5 VOCABULARY
Connecting ideas formally

A These expressions connect ideas in different ways. Put them in the correct columns. Sometimes more than one answer is possible.

| additionally | as a result | for instance | in fact | nevertheless | similarly |
| as a matter of fact | for example | furthermore | likewise | on the other hand | therefore |

Add information	Compare or contrast	Emphasize	Give an example	Show a result
additionally				

B Choose the appropriate connector to complete the sentences.

1. Tom loves technology; *similarly / for example*, he has the latest cell phone.
2. Many airports offer inexpensive Wi-Fi; *nevertheless / in fact*, at some it's even free.
3. Many of my friends' computers have been damaged by viruses; *nevertheless / therefore*, I am going to update my antivirus software.
4. Some websites aren't reliable; *as a result / likewise*, many people are being misinformed.
5. Few people could have predicted recent advances in Internet technology; *for example / likewise*, predicting the future of the Internet is difficult.
6. Internet identity theft is something very serious; *on the other hand / as a matter of fact*, it can ruin your life.

VOCABULARY PLUS see page 136

6 DISCUSSION
Social networking debate

A **Pair work** Do you think social networking sites are a positive or negative influence? Find a partner who has the same opinion.

B **Group work** Find a pair who disagrees with you and your partner. Take turns explaining your reasons. Each pair gets a chance to disagree.

"The way I see it, social networking sites are a positive influence because they allow me to have friends all over the world."

"That may be true, but in my opinion, online friends aren't really true friends. In fact, . . ."

Useful expressions		
Expressing opinions	**Disagreeing**	**Giving reasons**
If you ask me, . . .	That may be true, but . . .	That's why . . .
The way I see it, . . .	I see your point, but . . .	The reason for that is . . .

56 UNIT 7 The information age

7 WRITING
Writing a product or service review

> Writing and posting a product or service review helps other consumers make informed decisions. Most product and service reviews contain similar features.

A Look at the information about product reviews. Then read the review below and select the things the review does. Find examples in the review with a partner.

- ☐ 1. names the product and explains its use
- ☐ 2. explains where it can be purchased
- ☐ 3. mentions positive features
- ☐ 4. suggests how it could be improved
- ☐ 5. states who would find it useful and why
- ☐ 6. gives the exact price

Organize Me XPS is one of the best tools I have used for managing my busy schedule – and I have used many over the years. With this app, I'm able to organize all of my tasks and appointments in one place with just a couple of simple steps. Furthermore, a simple set-up is all it takes to share my plans with others. Having the ability to share my lists and calendars with colleagues and friends like this is extremely useful.

The only drawback some people might find is that it does not have all of the features offered by some of the more expensive productivity apps; nevertheless, it does exactly what I need it to do. In fact, the app's simplicity is its best feature. I just love the simple interface. Although the developers promise that free updates offering new features will be released soon, if you ask me, the low cost makes it a really good value as is.

If you're someone who writes notes on little pieces of paper and then loses them, get this app. It will really boost your productivity. I use it every day – for school, work, and everything else.

B Use one of these topics or your own idea to write a product or service review.

- technology you purchased
- a game or app you tried
- a restaurant you ate at
- a service you used (dry cleaner, hair salon, mechanic)

C Group work Take turns reading your reviews. Then answer the questions.

1. Whose review is the most interesting and informative? Why?
2. What additional information would you want to know as a consumer?
3. Which reviews would convince you to buy the product or use the service? Which ones would lead you to make a different choice?

LESSON B ▶ Information overload

1 STARTING POINT
Future shock

A Read these comments about technology. Do you agree or disagree?

WHAT'S Your TAKE ON TECHNOLOGY?

Joo-chan, Seoul:
"Apps are cool, aren't they? I download lots of them to my smartphone. Wouldn't it be great if phones came loaded with even more apps?"

Ana, São Paulo:
"Isn't it weird how some people use mobile devices constantly? They don't notice anything around them. It's actually dangerous, don't you think?"

Sarah, Los Angeles:
"Don't you think there are too many websites full of misinformation? Shouldn't the government fine sites that contain false information?"

Yang Ming, Taipei:
"Doesn't it seem like kids spend too much time playing violent video games? It makes kids more aggressive, doesn't it?"

B Pair work Compare your answers with a partner. Do you think the government should regulate any of these things?

2 VOCABULARY
Forms of communication

A Where do you find these forms of communication? Put them in the correct columns. Then add another expression to each category.

| banner ads | bumper stickers | crawls | infomercials | spam | text messages |
| billboards | bus wraps | fliers | pop-up ads | telemarketing | voice mail |

On television	On the Internet	On the phone	On streets or highways

B Pair work Which of the above are the most useful ways of communicating information? The least useful? Do you find any of them annoying?

"Those crawls at the bottom of TV screens aren't useful. It's impossible to read them and pay attention to a show at the same time. Don't you think they're annoying?"

VOCABULARY PLUS see page 136

58   UNIT 7   The information age

3 GRAMMAR

Negative and tag questions for giving opinions

Use negative questions or tag questions to offer an opinion and invite someone to react.
Isn't it weird how some people use mobile devices constantly?
Doesn't it seem like kids spend too much time playing violent video games?
Wouldn't it be great if phones came loaded with even more apps?
Shouldn't the government fine sites that contain false information?
Apps are cool, **aren't they**?
It makes kids more aggressive, **doesn't it**?

Use the phrase *don't you think* to form negative or tag questions for opinions.
Don't you think there are too many websites full of misinformation?
It's actually dangerous, **don't you think**?

GRAMMAR PLUS *see page 119*

A Look at the Starting Point on page 58 again. Find the tag questions used by Joo-chan and Yang Ming. Why do they have different endings?

B Pair work Turn the statements into negative or tag questions. Then ask and answer the questions. Discuss your answers.

1. It's annoying how often telemarketers call.
2. They should get rid of those banner ads on the Internet.
3. It would be great if there were fewer billboards.
4. It seems like a lot of people are texting while driving.
5. It's sad when people are tricked into losing money by spam messages.
6. There are too many channels on TV these days.

4 DISCUSSION

It's kind of strange, isn't it?

A Pair work Do you agree or disagree with these opinions? Why?

- Millions of people are addicted to online games these days. It's kind of sad, isn't it?
- Wouldn't it be great if the Internet were turned off one day a week to give people a chance to rest?
- Don't you think a lot of people are being confused by misinformation on the Internet?
- Aren't kids today being exposed to too much information on television and on the Internet?
- Don't you find it annoying that social networking sites sell your personal information to marketers?

B Group work What other problems are caused by modern information technology? Agree on the three most pressing problems and tell the class.

"Don't you think kids today spend too much time online? Won't their grades and social development suffer because of it?"

"You might be right. But their parents should set limits for them, shouldn't they?"

LESSON B Information overload

5 LISTENING
Health and technology

A Listen to a report on health problems caused by technology. Who is the main intended audience? Choose the correct answer.

☐ a. doctors or other health professionals
☐ b. frequent users of technology products
☐ c. designers of computers and mobile devices

B Listen again and complete the chart.

Problem	Symptoms	Advice
texter's thumb		
carpal tunnel syndrome		
gadget addiction		

6 DISCUSSION
Future technologies?

A Read about these technologies. Are any of them available now? Do you think any will be available in the future? Would you like to make use of them? Why or why not?

Technologies of Tomorrow?

You'll never be bored with the color of your clothes or furniture again. With color-changing fabric, you'll be able to select from a wide variety of colors using a remote control, changing colors whenever you want.

Wireless electricity will allow you to do away with chargers, batteries, and cords. Devices and appliances in homes and businesses will run on electricity transmitted wirelessly from a hidden power source.

A life recorder is a small wearable device that will take a video of everything you see, twenty-four hours a day, seven days a week. The sights and sounds of your entire life will be saved for years to come.

B **Group work** What new technologies are becoming popular? Which ones do you think are useful? What other technologies do you think will be invented in the future?

7 READING
Cyber-begging

A **Pair work** Imagine that a stranger asked you for money to help pay off a frivolous debt. Would you help? Tell your partner. Then read the article.

Can you spare a dime for my Gucci bills?

There was a time when Karyn Bosnak couldn't pay a $59.00 bill at the grocery store. She was officially broke. She didn't have enough money to get on the subway, but she looked rich. She was a television producer, earned $900 a week, and had a closetful of designer labels like Gucci and Louis Vuitton. But she also had a $20,221.40 credit card bill and an empty bank account. Karyn decided that it was time for a change. She built a website and simply asked people to help her out by sending her a buck or two.

On the site, Karyn honestly explained her situation, Gucci shoes and all. "If 20,000 people gave me just $1, I'd be home free, and I'm sure there are 20,000 people out there who can afford to give me $1." Amazingly, it worked. Her website was visited by more than a million people. Although most donors just gave a few dollars, one generous donor sent $1,000. She was on TV and in newspapers and magazines. She was offered a book deal and a movie contract. And of course, she was able to pay off her credit card debt.

She also sold her designer clothes on eBay. In her closet, where the Gucci purses once sat, Karyn keeps all the letters that people have sent her. She's received teddy bears, subscriptions to *Vogue*, Dunkin' Donuts coupons, backpacks, jewelry, cat food, and candles.

It's hard to understand why so many people helped a total stranger pay off her huge credit card bill. Why did they do it? Karyn explains, "I was just honest about what happened; I didn't make up some sob story about saving the world." Her donors think it's funny and original, she argues, and view it less as a charity than as an entertainment site.

Imitators have sprung up all over the Internet, some with outrageously selfish requests like a BMW or a house. Actually, Karyn was not the first person to put up a website asking strangers for money. The practice has a name: "cyber-begging." Most sites receive little traffic and even less cash.

Karyn also had thousands of enemies and critics. People sent her hate mail and scolded her on websites. Karyn says she never let this anger bother her. "They are probably jealous they didn't think of it," she explains.

Source: "Brother, can you spare a dime for my Gucci bills?" by Janelle Brown, Salon.com

B Read the article again and answer the questions. Then compare your answers with a partner.

1. Why was Karyn in financial trouble?
2. What was her main solution to her problem? What else did she do?
3. Why did so many people respond positively to her website?

C **Group work** Discuss these questions. Then share your answers with the class.

1. Do you think Karyn was unethical, or was she simply clever?
2. What would you have done if you were Karyn?

8 PUTTING THE MIND TO WORK

LESSON A ▶ Exploring creativity

1 STARTING POINT
Creative professions

A Pair work How much creativity do you think these jobs require? Number them from 1 (most creative) to 4 (least creative). Explain your choices.

____ chef   ____ surgeon   ____ photographer   ____ jazz musician

"I think a chef has to be the most creative. Inventing new dishes requires a lot of creativity."

B Group work Which jobs might be right for these kinds of people? Discuss your answers.

1. someone able to think quickly
2. a person looking for adventure
3. people good with their hands
4. someone needing job security
5. a person trained in music
6. a person with a good voice

"Someone able to think quickly might be a good surgeon. You never know what might go wrong once the operation starts."

2 VOCABULARY
Creative qualities

A What qualities do creative people usually have? Complete the chart with the correct nouns or adjectives.

Noun	Adjective	Noun	Adjective	Noun	Adjective
curiosity	*curious*	innovation			passionate
decisiveness		knowledge		patience	
	determined		motivated		perceptive
	disciplined		original		resourceful

B Pair work Which of the qualities in the chart are most important to your job or studies? Discuss with a partner.

"Well, I'm studying engineering, and we get a lot of assignments, so I have to be very disciplined. It's a very competitive field."

VOCABULARY PLUS see page 137

UNIT 8 Putting the mind to work

3 GRAMMAR
Reduced relative clauses

You can shorten a relative clause by dropping the relative pronoun and the verb *be*.
Someone (**who / that is**) **able to think quickly** might be a good surgeon.
A person (**who / that is**) **looking for adventure** could be a private detective.
A person (**who / that is**) **trained in music** might be a good DJ.

You can also drop *who / that* and change the verb to the gerund.
Someone **who / that needs job security** might not want to be a jazz musician.
Someone **needing job security** might not want to be a jazz musician.

In many relative clauses, *who / that* + the verb *have* can be replaced by *with*.
A person **who / that has a good voice** could be a good TV journalist.
A person **with a good voice** could be a good TV journalist.

GRAMMAR PLUS *see page 120*

A Look at the Starting Point on page 62 again. Can you make the reduced relative clauses in part B into full clauses? What verb forms do the full clauses use?

B Rewrite these sentences with reduced relative clauses. Then compare with a partner.

1. Someone who hopes to be a chef should get the proper training.
   Someone hoping to be a chef should get the proper training.
2. Anyone who wants to be an actor needs both talent and luck.
3. A person who works as a comedian is always looking for new ways to make people laugh.
4. People who are clever enough to get inside the mind of a criminal would make good detectives.
5. Anyone who dreams of becoming a champion athlete has to be prepared to do a lot of hard work.
6. Someone who is interested in the latest music trends might be a good DJ.
7. A person who is responsible for a large staff has to be able to be creative with scheduling.

C Complete these sentences using reduced relative clauses and your own ideas.

1. . . . needs to take voice lessons.
   Someone dreaming of becoming a professional singer needs to take voice lessons.
2. . . . should speak English as much as possible.
3. . . . should keep up with current events.
4. . . . doesn't need to have a good speaking voice.
5. . . . should follow the latest trends in clothing.
6. . . . has to study the behavior of animals.
7. . . . usually have a great love of food and eating.
8. . . . will find the job market extremely competitive.

LESSON A Exploring creativity

4 DISCUSSION
Creativity quiz

A How creative are you? Complete the quiz.

How Creative Are You?

	Always	Sometimes	Rarely	Never
1. Are you a risk taker?	3	2	1	0
2. Are you naturally curious?	3	2	1	0
3. Do you look for opportunities to improve things?	3	2	1	0
4. Are you sensitive to beauty?	3	2	1	0
5. Do you challenge accepted ideas?	3	2	1	0
6. Do you keep an eye out for new fashions and products?	3	2	1	0
7. Do you adapt easily to new situations?	3	2	1	0
8. Do you trust your guesses, intuitions, and insights?	3	2	1	0
9. Are you more interested in the future than in the past?	3	2	1	0
10. Do you have a creative sense of humor?	3	2	1	0

B **Pair work** Add up your score. Then check what your score means below. Do you agree? Why or why not? Tell your partner.

	21–30	11–20	0–10
About You	Because you're open-minded, you like to keep up with the latest trends and innovations. Accepting the status quo bores you. You see mistakes as learning experiences.	You often have good ideas, but you prefer to feel them out with friends before taking action. You're up-to-date with new fashions and products, but unlikely to be the first in your group to try them.	You prefer to stick with the tried-and-true, which helps you feel safe, but you may get left behind in later years. You're content with who you are and what you know.

5 LISTENING
Creativity at work

🔊 **A** Listen to Samira, Alex, and Naomi talking about their occupations. What does each person do?

🔊 **B** Listen again. What do Samira (S), Alex (A), and Naomi (N) say they focus on in their work? Write the correct letter.

____ 1. helping indecisive clients   ____ 4. solving a wide variety of problems
____ 2. efficiency   ____ 5. new ideas to replace rejected ones
____ 3. beating the competition   ____ 6. using old concepts in new ways

6 WRITING
Beginning new paragraphs

Begin a new paragraph each time you change the focus of your ideas.

A Read this composition. The writer changes focus twice. Indicate with a *P* where the two new paragraphs should begin. Then compare answers with a partner.

Lucy Gomez is the most creative person I know. She started piano lessons when she was only four years old. At school, she was always creating interesting projects in her art class. When she was only 12 years old, she won a citywide poetry contest. Her parents were very proud of her. Lucy works as a sitcom writer for a popular TV show now. She works with a group of writers, and together they have to think of original ideas for stories. They also have to come up with funny dialogue for the actors on their show, because the actors have to play believable characters that will make the audience laugh. It is not an easy job, but Lucy does it well. She starts work late in the morning and often works until 7:00 or 8:00 at night. Lucy is very curious. She likes to travel and meet new people who have opinions that are different from hers. And she's always noting ideas, drawing quick sketches, and taking photos. She tells me that doing these things helps her turn new experiences into a source of ideas for her work. I always enjoy talking to her and am happy to know someone as knowledgeable and creative as Lucy.

B Brainstorm ideas for a composition about someone who is very creative or who is unique or different in an interesting way. Answer these questions to help you.

1. In what ways is this person special or different?
2. How does this affect his or her life?
3. Would you like to be like this person? Why or why not?

C Write a three-paragraph composition based on your ideas.

D **Pair work** Read your partner's composition and answer these questions.

1. Do the paragraphs start and end where they should?
2. Is the focus of each paragraph clear?
3. Is there any additional information you would like to know that was not included?

LESSON A Exploring creativity

LESSON B ▶ Ideas that work

1 STARTING POINT
Everyday objects

A Read about these unusual uses of everyday objects. Have you ever used them in these ways?

Three Clever Ideas

1 "I have three cats, which means there's usually a lot of cat fur on my clothes. To get rid of the fur, I wrap my hand in tape, sticky side out. Then I rub the tape over my clothes, and it picks up the fur!"

2 "The zipper was stuck on my favorite jacket. Luckily, my roommate works in fashion, which is great because she knew how to fix it. She just rubbed a drop of olive oil on the zipper."

3 "Tacos can be messy to eat, which is why I wrap them in paper coffee filters. I serve them that way at parties and backyard barbecues. It works great for other messy sandwiches, too!"

B **Group work** Use your imagination to suggest new uses for these everyday items. Decide on the best use for each and share it with the class.

- old newspapers
- a shower curtain
- aluminum foil
- empty shoe boxes
- dental floss
- a hair dryer
- empty jars or cans
- rubber bands

"You can wrap green tomatoes in newspaper to make them ripen more quickly."

2 VOCABULARY & SPEAKING
Exploring possibilities

A Combine the verbs with the nouns to make common expressions.

Verbs			Nouns			
analyze	find	organize	a decision	a problem	a solution	possibilities
explore	make	solve	a mistake	a situation	alternatives	information

analyze a situation, solve a problem, . . .

B **Pair work** Discuss the questions. Then ask your partner more questions using the new vocabulary.

1. When do you make decisions quickly? When do you explore the possibilities first?
2. Who do you talk to when you need to find a solution to a big problem? Why?
3. When was the last time you analyzed a mistake you made? What did you learn from it?

VOCABULARY PLUS *see page 137*

3 GRAMMAR

Non-defining relative clauses as sentence modifiers

You can use non-defining relative clauses with *which* to make a comment about an entire sentence.
I have three cats, **which means there's usually a lot of cat fur on my clothes**.
My roommate is a slob, **which is why I want to get my own apartment**.

GRAMMAR PLUS see page 121

A Look at the Starting Point on page 66 again. Can you find more examples of these grammar patterns? How are the commas used?

B Match these statements with the appropriate non-defining clauses. Then compare with a partner and write two similar statements of your own.

1. I want to give away all my old books, _h_
2. I had locked my keys in my car, ___
3. I've been exploring possibilities for natural cleaners, ___
4. My son made a robot costume for himself, ___
5. Our neighbor saves her empty jars for my dad, ___
6. I downloaded a great new app that helps me organize information, ___
7. It's easy to get lost when driving in a new city, ___
8. Adam has bought some expensive software to edit videos, ___

a. which is why you saw me opening it with a coat hanger.
b. which is great since he uses them to store nails and things in his workroom.
c. which is great because I think it's solved my problem of forgetting where I store files.
d. which is why I was wiping lemon juice and salt on those copper pots.
e. which is one reason why GPS systems were developed for cars.
f. which is why he was covered in aluminum foil yesterday.
g. which is strange since there are plenty of free programs that do that well.
h. which means I have to get boxes for them.

4 SPEAKING

Key inventions

A What inventions or discoveries do you think have had the greatest impact on modern life? Make a list.

the cell phone   *the television*   *the airplane*

B Group work Compare lists with your group.

"I think the cell phone has really affected people's lives. People can talk wherever they are, which means they can always be in touch and save time."

LESSON B Ideas that work 67

5 LISTENING
Great ideas

A Look at the pictures. What do you know about these products or services? How do you think they were developed?

B Listen to these stories about the invention and development of the products in the photos. Complete the chart.

	Bill Bowerman	Fred Smith
How he got the idea		
The initial reaction to the idea		
What the inventor did in response		

6 DISCUSSION
Making life better

A **Pair work** Why do people create or invent new products? Read this list of reasons and add two more of your own.

- to help protect people's health
- to make business more efficient
- to make daily life easier
- to make life more enjoyable
- to protect the environment
- to save lives
- _____
- _____

B **Group work** Join another pair. Why do you think these things were created or invented? Use the reasons in part A or others of your own.

1. air conditioners
2. artificial sweeteners
3. digital cameras
4. electric knives
5. hybrid cars
6. karaoke machines
7. laptops
8. lie detectors
9. scanners

"I think air conditioners were invented to protect people's health. The summer heat can be deadly for infants and the elderly."

UNIT 8 Putting the mind to work

7 READING

A unique inventor and his invention

A Read the title of the article. What do you think Daisuke Inoue invented? Then read the article and check your answer.

The Man Who Taught the World to Sing

Daisuke Inoue was a drummer in a band near Osaka, Japan, that played versions of famous pop songs. People loved to sing along as the band played, but most of them couldn't carry a tune. Inoue's band had spent years learning how to make the untalented customer sound in tune by adjusting the music to match the customer's voice. The singers, mainly Japanese businessmen out for a night on the town, loved Inoue's unique follow-along style.

In 1971, a loyal client asked Inoue to escort him on a company trip, but Inoue could not attend. He found a solution: he recorded his band's back-up tracks, and then hooked up a car stereo and an amplifier. With this device, Inoue gave birth to the karaoke machine. By the 1980s, *karaoke*, which means "empty orchestra," was a Japanese word that required no translation across the globe.

Unfortunately, Inoue never bothered to patent the world's first karaoke machine, so he lost his chance to become one of Japan's richest men. When asked if he regretted not patenting his invention, 65-year-old Daisuke Inoue confessed, "I'm not an inventor. I am just resourceful. I simply put things that already exist together. Who would consider patenting something like that?"

Inoue's friend Robert Scott Field says, "Some people say he lost 150 million dollars. If it were me, I'd be crying in the corner, but he's a happy guy. I think he's amazed to find that he's touched so many lives." Inoue believes the little box he put together has had a huge social impact, especially in Japan. At weddings and company get-togethers, the karaoke comes out and people relax. It breaks the ice.

Although Inoue spent years in obscurity, in 1999, *Time* magazine called him one of the twentieth century's most influential people, saying he had "helped to liberate the once unvoiced."

Inoue is always getting asked silly questions, but he takes them in stride. "Women approach me all the time and ask if I can help their husbands sing better. I always say that if her husband were any good at singing, he would be making a living at it. He's bad, which means he's just like the rest of us."

Inoue didn't use a modern karaoke machine until he was 59 years old, but his favorite English songs are "Love Is a Many Splendored Thing" and Ray Charles' "I Can't Stop Loving You." "They're easy, which is good because I'm a terrible singer," said Daisuke Inoue, the man who taught the world to sing.

Source: "Mr. Song and Dance Man," by Dr. David McNeill, Sophia University, Tokyo

B Group work Discuss these questions. Then share your answers with the class.

1. What led Daisuke Inoue to create his invention? Do you agree he was only being resourceful, or was he actually an inventor? Explain.
2. Would you have the same attitude as Inoue if you invented something popular and received no compensation? Why or why not?
3. How do you think Inoue "helped to liberate the once unvoiced" both as a drummer in his band and as the inventor of karaoke? Do you think this is a good thing? Explain.

9 GENERALLY SPEAKING
LESSON A ▶ How typical are you?

1 STARTING POINT
What's typical?

A Read about the "typical" person in Italy and Japan. What information surprised you? Why?

The typical ITALIAN person . . .	The typical JAPANESE person . . .
drinks **155 liters** of bottled water per year.	drinks **10 liters** of bottled water per year.
consumes **3.2 kilograms** of coffee per year.	consumes **1.4 kilograms** of coffee per year.
consumes **0.1 kilograms** of tea per year.	consumes **0.9 kilograms** of tea per year.
visits the doctor **6 times** per year.	visits the doctor **14 times** per year.
watches **27 hours** of TV per week.	watches **21 hours** of TV per week.
gets married at **30 years old** (for men) or **27 years old** (for women).	gets married at **30 years old** (for men) or **27 years old** (for women).
studies for **7.2 years** after the age of 15.	studies for **9.5 years** after the age of 15.
travels **710 kilometers** by rail per year.	travels **1,900 kilometers** by rail per year.

Source: www.nationmaster.com

B Complete these statements. Use information from the chart.

1. Unlike the Japanese, Italians seem to drink a lot of _**bottled water**_.
2. While the typical _____ person studies until the age of 22, the typical _____ person studies until the age of 24.
3. Both like TV, except that the typical _____ person watches more.
4. In contrast to Italians, the Japanese travel a lot more _____.
5. Both groups are fairly different, except for the age _____.

2 SPEAKING
That's just so typical!

A Pair work What are typical examples of these things in your hometown?

1. a store   2. a home   3. a job   4. a car   5. a snack food   6. a weekend activity

B Group work Join another pair and compare your answers.

"What's a typical store in your hometown?"
"We have something called 'dollar stores.' They have household goods, clothes, toys, and lots of other stuff. And everything's really inexpensive."

3 GRAMMAR

Clauses and phrases showing contrast and exception

Use *while*, *unlike*, and *in contrast to* in order to present contrasting information, especially in writing.
While the typical Italian person studies until the age of 22, the typical Japanese person studies until the age of 24.
Unlike the Japanese, Italians seem to drink a lot of bottled water.
In contrast to Italians, the Japanese travel a lot more by rail.

Use *except* (*that*), *except* (*for*), and *except for the fact* (*that*) to show an exception.
Both like TV, **except** (**that**) the typical Italian person watches more.
Italian and Japanese people are fairly different, **except for** the age they get married.
Japanese people typically consume less, **except for the fact that** they drink more tea.

GRAMMAR PLUS see page 122

A Look at the Starting Point on page 70 again. Notice the sentences in part B that use phrases with *except*. Which phrase is followed by a clause?

B Here's some information about customs. How are they different in other places? Write sentences showing contrasts and indicating exceptions.

1. When people in the U.S. go to a party, they usually arrive a few minutes late.
   Unlike people in the U.S., most people where I live arrive on time for parties.
2. Most people in Canada have cereal and milk for breakfast some days of the week.
3. Most people in the U.S. who study a foreign language in college choose Spanish.
4. In the U.K., it's common for friends to split the bill at a restaurant.
5. For people in Italy, lunch is the main meal of the day.
6. Women in Spain usually kiss people on both cheeks when they meet.

C Are you typical? Complete these sentences and compare with a partner.

1. Unlike most people where I live, *I don't own a car.*
2. In contrast to most of my friends, . . .
3. While a lot of the people where I live . . .
4. I'm similar to many of my friends, except that . . .

4 DISCUSSION

Are you typical?

Group work Choose the answer that makes each sentence true for you. Then compare answers with your group. Are you typical in your group?

Are you typical?

1. I need *six or less / seven / eight or more* hours of sleep.
2. For commuting, I rely mainly on *buses / subways / trains / taxis / a car*.
3. I tend to eat *healthy / unhealthy snacks* between meals.
4. I spend the most time with my friends *in person / on the phone / online*.
5. I button my clothes from the *top down / bottom up*.
6. A great night out should include a *movie / play / concert / sporting event*.

"Unlike most of the people in my group, I need eight or more hours of sleep or I don't feel rested. Most people in my group need only six hours or less."

LESSON A How typical are you?

5 VOCABULARY
Should I just go with the flow?

A Are these adjectives, verbs, and phrases related to accepting things as they are or to making changes? Put them in the correct columns.

Adjectives	Verbs	Phrases
amenable	accept	be your own person
conservative	conform (to)	fit in
rebellious	confront	follow the crowd
(un)conventional	stand up (to/for)	make waves

Accepting things as they are	Making changes

B Group work Use the expressions in the chart in part A to describe what you think these people might be like. Give examples to explain your ideas.

1. Ed, a guy who gets along with everyone
2. Clarissa, an actor desperate for attention
3. Rob, an assistant at a law firm hoping for a promotion
4. Diana, a leader who wants to change the world

"Ed is probably amenable and does what other people want. I imagine he only confronts people if he really has to and generally follows the crowd."

VOCABULARY PLUS see page 138

6 LISTENING & SPEAKING
How are they different?

A Listen to Yoshiko, Diego, and Suzanne talking about their school experiences. Answer the questions.

1. What examples does Yoshiko give for how she is typical? In what way is she different?
2. What are three ways that Diego's life is typical? In what way doesn't he follow the crowd?
3. Does Suzanne give an example of how her life is unconventional? If so, what is it?

B Listen again. Do Yoshiko, Diego, and Suzanne believe they are typical or different from most people their age?

C Pair work Do you tend to go with the flow or be your own person? Discuss these questions.

1. Are your interests similar to those of your friends and family or different? Explain.
2. In what ways do the clothes you wear make you stand out or fit in?
3. How does your taste in music compare to that of other people your age?

Yoshiko in Mexico

7 WRITING
Supporting statements

> Supporting statements develop the topic sentence by providing key facts, reasons, or examples.

A Read the paragraph. What's the topic sentence? Underline three supporting statements that develop the main idea in the topic sentence. Then compare your answers with a partner.

Unconventionally Cool: Trendspotter Josie Buchier

June 13

My friend Josie Buchier doesn't like to follow the crowd. While most of us are trying our best to fit in with everyone else, Josie likes to be her own person. For instance, she has her own unique sense of fashion, so she likes to buy all her clothes, except for her shoes, in used clothing shops. Her taste in music is also pretty unconventional. Unlike most of my friends, she can't stand pop music. She prefers to listen to Philippine and Andean folk music. She also has a very interesting job. Unlike her old nine-to-five job in a conservative department store, she now works as a trendspotter for an advertising company. This means that she spends her time looking at the latest fashion and entertainment trends among young people. Then she writes reports for her company about what's in style. This makes my unconventional friend a trendsetter that others follow, and that's pretty cool.

[4 comments]

B Finish these statements with information of your own to make topic sentences. Compare with a partner.

1. Generally speaking, most people where I live don't . . .
2. One of my best friends is . . .
3. In general, my friends tend to be . . .

C Choose one of the topic sentences and brainstorm supporting ideas. Then choose at least four supporting statements and write a paragraph.

Generally speaking, most people where I live don't mind making waves. It's their way of . . .

D **Pair work** Exchange paragraphs and answer these questions.

1. Do all the supporting statements relate to the topic sentence?
2. Do they develop and explain the topic sentence?
3. Do the supporting details fit together in a logical order?
4. What other facts, reasons, or examples could be added?

LESSON B ▸ Problems and solutions

1 STARTING POINT
I never used to feel stressed.

A Read Annie's email to her friend. What problems does she have?

To: Adriana Costa
From: Annie Wilson
Subject: Missing you!

Hi Adriana,

How are things back in Cartagena? Are you glad to be home again? Sorry I haven't written lately. I have a lot of new responsibilities at work now, so I've been really stressed. My job didn't use to be so demanding!

I have to say, I miss you. You used to be such a good influence on me! These days, I oversleep. I'm even late for work sometimes! That never used to happen because I knew I had to meet you at the café in the morning. I remember how you would complain about the coffee they served. You used to call it "brown water"!

I'm spending too much money, too. Every time I go to the mall, I see something I want to buy. That's another reason I miss you! I would see some great jacket, but you wouldn't let me buy it. You would always tell me I didn't need it and drag me away!

Also, I have a noisy new roommate, Cindy. All she ever does is gab on her cell! Remember the way we would sit around talking? You always used to make me laugh. I bet that's a big reason I never used to feel stressed like I do now!

Anyway, the weekend will be here soon, so I'm sure I'll feel better then.

Write soon!

Annie

B Pair work What do you think Annie should do about her problems?

"Annie should find another friend to meet at the café in the morning."

2 VOCABULARY
Expressions with *keep* and *stay*

A Match the phrases to make questions. Notice the expressions with *keep* and *stay*.

1. When you're stressed, can you **keep** __e__
2. When friends move away, do you **keep / stay** ____
3. If you're sleepy while studying, what can you do to **stay** ____
4. What news sources do you read in order to **keep** ____
5. Do you break the rules or do you **keep / stay** ____
6. How do you save money when you need to **keep** ____
7. Is it important for old friends to **keep / stay** ____

a. expenses down?
b. up with current events?
c. connected?
d. in touch?
e. things in perspective?
f. awake?
g. out of trouble?

B Pair work Take turns answering the questions. Discuss your answers.

VOCABULARY PLUS see page 138

UNIT 9 Generally speaking

3 GRAMMAR

Past habitual with *used to* and *would*

Used to and *would* can both be used to describe past habitual actions or situations which are no longer true. However, *would* cannot be used with stative verbs such as *live*, *be*, *have*, or *like*.

You always **used to make** me laugh.
My job **didn't use to be** so demanding!
Remember the way we **would sit** around talking?
I **would see** some great jacket, but you **wouldn't let** me buy it.

GRAMMAR PLUS see page 123

A Look at the Starting Point on page 74 again. Make a list of the things that have changed for Annie since Adriana went back to Colombia.

B Complete these sentences with *used to* or *would*. Sometimes more than one answer is possible.

The first year of high school, I wasn't a very good student. I (1) ____used to____ think school was boring. I remember my classmates (2) _____ go to the library and work on projects or study, but I (3) _____ like to play video games at a friend's house instead. We (4) _____ go right after class, and we (5) _____ spend three or four hours doing that. My parents both (6) _____ have jobs with long hours, so they never knew what time I (7) _____ get home. I thought I was smart, and that I didn't need to study to keep my grades up. But one day, I was asked to go to the principal's office. He said, "You (8) _____ be a great student. Now your grades are terrible. Explain!" That was a real wake-up call. After that, I became serious about school, and I (9) _____ study and finish my homework before playing video games. Now that my kids are in high school, I tell them about all the silly things I (10) _____ do when I was their age.

4 DISCUSSION

Personal concerns

A **Pair work** These people have had a change in their lives. What positive or negative impacts have these changes had?

Lucas Santos, 25, Curitiba
"Before my wife and I had our first baby, we would go out whenever we wanted. We can't do that now. I didn't use to be a worrier, but I am now."

Britney Majors, 32, Toronto
"Before my promotion, I would eat lunch in the cafeteria because that was all I could afford. Now I have money to go to nice cafés, but I just don't have the time. So, I usually eat at my desk."

Wen Ho Chen, 67, Taipei
"We used to plan on moving in with our son when we retired. But we've changed our minds. We just sold our house, and we're going to travel the world."

B **Group work** Think about a big change in your life. Talk about the positive and negative impacts it had.

"Last year, I was transferred to another department in my company. My new responsibilities are a lot more interesting, but I didn't use to have to work this much."

LESSON B Problems and solutions

5 LISTENING & SPEAKING
Different approaches to problem solving

A **Pair work** Read about these three approaches to problem solving. What method do you use? Give examples to support your answer.

What kind of problem solver are you?

Different people solve their problems in different ways. The three main approaches are assertive, meditative, and cooperative. Find out which one best describes you.

▶ **Assertive** people prefer action to talk. When they're faced with a problem, they immediately try to work out a solution.

▶ When **meditative** people have a problem, they sit and think about it, and might even do research. Sometimes, the answer comes to them if they don't act on something right away.

▶ **Cooperative** people think the easiest way to solve a problem is to ask for help. Another person's perspective can help cooperative people come up with solutions.

"I'd say I'm a meditative person. Before I bought my first car, I spent hours doing research on it by myself. It took me forever to decide!"

B Listen to Dominique, Carla, and Wayne talking about their personal concerns. What kind of problem solver is each person?

C Listen again. What are two things each person did to solve their problem?

6 ROLE PLAY
Here's an idea . . .

A Read about these people's problems. What advice would you give each person?

- My boss is so demanding. She gives me more work than I can handle.
- I can't save money because I always spend it on little things I want but don't really need.
- My last job interview went very badly. I always get tongue-tied in front of authority figures.
- I'm not enjoying things like I used to. I'm not sure why. Maybe I'm too stressed.

B Role-play each situation. Take turns giving and receiving advice.

"My boss is so demanding. She gives me more work than I can handle."

"Here's an idea. See if your co-workers feel the same way. Maybe you all can talk to the boss about it."

"I guess I could try that."

Useful expressions	
Giving advice	**Receiving advice**
Here's an idea . . .	I guess I could try that.
If I were you, I'd . . .	I just might try that.

7 READING
Creative problem solving

A Pair work Look at these paintings of the same landscape. How are they different? What effect does this have on what you notice first? Discuss. Then read the article.

Painting and Problem Solving: FOUR LESSONS

Earlier this month I escaped the office for a weeklong painting retreat in the woods of Door County, Wisconsin. While working amidst the awe-inspiring fall colors, it occurred to me that the dynamics of painting and problem solving have a lot in common. I returned home not only with newly polished painting skills but also a fresh perspective on managing problems. I learned four lessons while painting:

1 How you see things depends on your line of sight. When painting a landscape, countless choices are yours. For starters, you can choose where to place the horizon and what you eliminate from the actual setting. If the existing landscape is cluttered, for instance, you can exclude elements that detract from your focal point. Likewise, in problem solving, getting caught up in the clutter diminishes your ability to reach your desired result. Choose instead to focus on the bigger picture.

2 People can see the same landscape and represent it in totally different ways. One day I sat with two other painters in a microclimate with magnificent sugar maples. Much to my surprise, our final paintings were totally different. A similar phenomenon occurs in problem solving: Any number of people can arrive at the same situation with different ideas, skills, or resources. They can also have different designs on the end result. In this way, respecting where others are coming from is critical to problem solving.

3 When light is shined on a subject, you can explore what lies in the shadows. It can be harder to paint landscapes on cloudy days. The various forms and contrasts are less clear, and it's difficult to explore what lies in the shadows. When the sun is shining, however, the distinctions between objects are clearly visible and what lies in the shadows is revealed. The same goes for problem solving: When you shine a light on an issue, you see everything more clearly, including what opportunities or threats exist in the shadows.

4 Collaborating with people at different levels can foster appreciation for diverse ideas and perspectives. At the retreat, there were painters at every level, from first-timers to fine artists. I learned something from each one, particularly when our group came in from the woods and worked together in the studio. I opened myself up to others' unique observations and feedback, and ultimately felt more energized and creative. Additionally, I was struck by our instructor's capacity to calibrate her critiques to our individual skill levels. Similarly, in problem solving, it's important to meet others where they are, not where you might want them to be.

Odds are there is a problem on your desk today. How might even one of these four lessons help you brush up your problem-solving skills?

Source: "4 Ways to Brush Up Your Problem-Solving Skills," by Barbara T. Armstrong

B Group work Discuss these questions. Then share your answers with the class.

1. In what way is it helpful to avoid paying attention to details when solving a problem?
2. How are the second and fourth lessons in the article similar?
3. What do you think the author means by "shine a light on an issue"? How is this helpful?
4. How can the lessons from the article help you solve one of your own problems?

COMMUNICATION REVIEW
UNITS 7–9

✓ SELF-ASSESSMENT

How well can you do these things? Choose the best answer.

I can . . .	Very well	OK	A little
▶ Describe how information technology has changed people's lives (Ex. 1)	☐	☐	☐
▶ Describe how new technologies will change people's lives (Ex. 2)	☐	☐	☐
▶ Understand the main points of a phone conversation about personality types (Ex. 3)	☐	☐	☐
▶ Describe my personality type (Ex. 3)	☐	☐	☐
▶ Describe and compare typical behavior of parents and teenagers (Ex. 4)	☐	☐	☐

Now do the corresponding exercises. Was your assessment correct?

1 DISCUSSION
How things have changed!

A Think about how information technology has changed in the past few years. How have people's shopping habits, hobbies, and social lives been affected?

B **Pair work** Compare your answers with a partner.

"Video games used to be low-tech and expensive. Some games used to be available on the Internet, but few people would play them. Now, a lot of people play video games online. I think they've been greatly improved, and many are fairly cheap."

"Yeah, I think so, too. But too much time is spent playing them. My whole family is addicted – even my grandmother plays! She used to think video games were a waste of time when I played them as a kid."

2 DISCUSSION
What next?

A **Pair work** What do you think will happen in the next 10 years as a result of new technologies in these areas?

1. communication
2. education
3. entertainment
4. finance
5. medicine
6. sports

B **Group work** Compare your predictions in groups.

"Ten years from now, I think cell phones will be used by everyone. They'll even be used at work instead of office phones. What do you think?"

3 LISTENING & SPEAKING
Team roles: The perfect "STEAM" team

A Listen to the phone conversation between Tony and Annie. What is Tony's agency doing? Choose the correct answer.

- ☐ a. They're exploring the possibilities of using cell phones in advertising.
- ☐ b. They're analyzing the effectiveness of their advertisements.
- ☐ c. They're working to improve a company's image.

B Listen again. Match the roles on the left with the personality types on the right.

Role	Personality type
1. Solver _d_	a. disciplined
2. Team manager ___	b. patient
3. Explorer ___	c. passionate
4. Analyst ___	d. creative
5. Motivator ___	e. resourceful

C **Pair work** Look at the roles again. Which role do you think you would be best at or would enjoy most? Why? Compare your ideas with a partner.

"I think I'd probably be best in an Explorer role. I'm pretty resourceful. What about you?"

"I'm a person with a lot of patience, but I'm not that creative. I'm more of a Team manager type."

4 SPEAKING
That's so typical!

A Complete this chart with your opinions about typical parents and teenagers.

	The typical parent	The typical teenager
What are some of their concerns?		
What is their most valued possession?		
How much time do they spend with friends?		
What do they use the Internet for?		
What do they like to do on vacation?		

B Write at least four sentences contrasting the typical parent with the typical teenager. Then compare with a partner.

"Generally, the typical teenager is concerned about friends, while the typical parent is concerned about his or her children."

10 THE ART OF COMPLAINING
LESSON A ▶ *That really bugs me!*

1 STARTING POINT
Everyday annoyances

A Have you ever had problems similar to these? Do you agree or disagree with these comments? Why?

"The thing that I hate is when kids ride their scooters on the sidewalk."

"One thing that bothers me is when my friends don't show up on time for things."

"Something that bugs me is people who take up two seats on a crowded bus."

"The thing I can't stand is co-workers who leave their cell phones ringing on their desks."

B Group work Look at the situations in part A. Would you complain, or would you be quietly annoyed? Why?

2 LISTENING & SPEAKING
It really irks me!

A Listen to Jane and Kyle talking about irritating situations. What bothered each person?

B Listen again. Discuss the questions.

1. Whose situation do you think was more annoying, Jane's or Kyle's?
2. Who do you think handled the situation better, Jane or Kyle?
3. How would you have reacted in each situation?

3 GRAMMAR

Relative clauses and noun clauses

A relative clause can occur in the subject or the object of a sentence.
Something **that bugs me** is people **who take up two seats on a crowded bus**.
The thing **(that) I can't stand** is co-workers **who / that leave their cell phones ringing on their desks**.

Some sentences use a relative clause and a noun clause beginning with a question word such as *when*.
The thing **(that) I hate** is **when kids ride their scooters on the sidewalk**.
One thing **that bothers me** is **when my friends don't show up on time for things**.

GRAMMAR PLUS see page 124

A Look at the Starting Point on page 80 again. Which clauses are relative clauses? Which are noun clauses?

B **Pair work** Complete the sentences with your own opinions. Then discuss them with a partner.

1. One thing that irks me about my neighbors is . . . *when they park too close to my car.*
2. Something that bothers me about my friends is . . .
3. If I'm riding in a car, something that irritates me is . . .
4. The thing that aggravates me most is a friend . . .
5. The thing that annoys me about people talking on cell phones is . . .
6. . . . is one thing that bothers me at home.

4 VOCABULARY

That drives me up the wall!

A Combine the verbs with the phrases. How many combinations can you make? How are their meanings different?

Verbs	Phrases			
drive	on someone's nerves	someone mad	someone upset
get	someone crazy	someone sick	someone's blood boil
make	someone down	someone up the wall	under someone's skin

B **Group work** How do these things make you feel? Discuss these situations using the expressions in part A.

1. people laughing at their own jokes
2. vending machines that "steal" your money
3. finding empty ice cube trays in the freezer
4. people eating on public transportation
5. airlines not serving food on long flights

"The thing that drives me crazy is when people laugh at their own jokes, and they're not funny!"

VOCABULARY PLUS see page 139

LESSON A That really bugs me!

5 DISCUSSION
Polite complaints

A Which of these descriptions fits you best? Give examples to support your answer.

I very rarely complain.	I only complain if I absolutely have to.	I complain because it's my right.	I complain about every little thing.
a silent sufferer	a calm, collected type	an activist	a whiner

"I guess I'm a silent sufferer. For example, I never complain in a restaurant, even if the food is awful."

"You don't? Bad food in a restaurant really annoys me. I always complain! I mean, why should I pay for terrible food? I guess I must be an activist."

B Pair work What would you do or say in these situations? Compare your answers.

1. A taxi driver is playing the radio loudly while you are trying to make a phone call.
2. Your neighbor's young son tore up all the flowers in your garden.
3. You see someone littering in a public park.

"If the taxi driver were playing the radio very loudly, I think I'd just speak louder. I probably wouldn't say anything to the driver. But I wouldn't give him a very good tip either."

6 ROLE PLAY
I hate to mention this, . . .

A Pair work Use the language in the box to create polite complaints for each situation. Then take turns acting out your complaints for the class.

1. You've been waiting in line for a long time, and someone suddenly cuts in front of you.
2. You've had a party, and one friend is still at your home long after everyone else has left. It's driving you up the wall because it's really late, and you need to get up early.
3. After you've been waiting patiently for your food for an hour, the waiter brings you the wrong order.
4. Every time you go out with your friend, she asks you to hold her belongings because she doesn't carry a bag. It's really beginning to get on your nerves.

Useful expressions

Complaining to strangers
Excuse me, but . . .
I'm sorry, but . . .

Complaining to friends/neighbors
I hate to mention this, but . . .
I'm sorry to bring this up, but . . .

B Group work Which complaints were the most effective? Which were the most polite?

7 WRITING
Messages of complaint

Writing an effective message of complaint is a powerful way to solve an ongoing problem with a product or service.

A Match the information to the points in the email.

> ### Writing an effective message of complaint
> An effective message of complaint about a purchase . . .
> 1. contains a clear subject line.
> 2. describes the product or service clearly.
> 3. explains the problem in detail.
> 4. mentions a receipt or other evidence.
> 5. explains exactly what you want.
> 6. provides contact information.

To: customerservice@phonegrp.cup.org
From: JM1990@cup.org
Subject: Damaged product — *1*

Dear Sir or Madam:

Last month, I ordered a smartphone, model number VG25S, from your website. When it arrived, I discovered that it was broken. The case was damaged, and the display screen was cracked.

At my own expense, I returned the phone to your service department over a month ago. I still have not received a replacement, nor has a customer service representative contacted me.

I have my credit card bill to prove I paid for this purchase, a one-year warranty, and a receipt from the post office. Therefore, I would like to receive a new phone as soon as possible.

Please call or email me about this matter. I look forward to your reply and hope you will handle this matter promptly.

Sincerely,

John Montgomery
101 Bee Tree Road
Encino, CA 91426
Phone: 310-555-2934

B Write an email complaining about one of these situations or one of your own.

- Your tablet came with the wrong battery charger, but you didn't notice until you brought it home. You called the store, and they refused to replace it.
- You bought airplane tickets in advance, but the airline had overbooked the flight, and you couldn't get on the plane.

C **Pair work** Take turns reading your emails. Did your partner follow all the steps for writing an effective message of complaint?

LESSON A That really bugs me! 83

LESSON B ▶ Let's do something about it!

1 STARTING POINT
Why don't they do something about it?

A How many of these problems have you experienced? Compare with a partner.

"Overcrowded buses really make me mad. I wonder why they don't have more buses at rush hour."

"Umbrellas are so poorly made these days. I don't know why they always break in the wind."

"My cell phone never works around here. I can't understand why the reception is so bad."

For service in English, press 1.

"Automated phone menus drive me crazy. What I don't get is why companies don't have people answer their phones."

"The clothes in those shops are unbelievably expensive. How anyone can afford them is beyond me."

"The college course I want is really popular. My big concern is whether I'll be able to get into the class."

B **Pair work** Which of the problems in part A bother you the most? Explain.

"Broken umbrellas definitely bother me the most. That happened to me just the other day."
"You can say that again. I just hate it when that happens."

> **Useful expressions**
>
> **Agreeing and showing sympathy**
> I know (exactly) what you mean.
> Yeah, I hate that too.
> You can say that again.

2 LISTENING
If this is correct, say, "Yes."

A Have you ever had problems with automated phone menus? What happened?

🔊 **B** Listen to Gabriel using an automated phone menu. Is he successful? Choose the best summary.

☐ a. He completed his business successfully and will pick up his prescription this evening.
☐ b. He can't fill his prescription because the machine didn't recognize what he said.
☐ c. His pronunciation is so poor that the system didn't understand anything he said.

🔊 **C** Listen again. Answer the questions.

1. What's the name of the store?
2. What is his prescription number?
3. What is his phone number?
4. What time does he want to pick up his prescription?

84 UNIT 10 The art of complaining

3 GRAMMAR

Simple and complex indirect questions

Simple indirect questions use statement word order and begin with expressions such as *I wonder*, *I'd like to know*, or *I can't understand*.

Why don't they have more buses at rush hour?   I wonder why **they don't have** more buses at rush hour.

Complex indirect questions also use statement word order. In addition, they begin or end with clauses or phrases with *be*.

Will I be able to get into the class?   **My big concern is** whether I'll be able to get into the class.
How can anyone afford them?   How anyone can afford them **is beyond me**.

GRAMMAR PLUS see page 125

A Look at the Starting Point on page 84 again. Can you find more indirect questions? Which ones are simple indirect questions? Which are complex?

B Rewrite these questions using the words in parentheses. Then compare answers with a partner.

1. Will airlines ever stop losing passengers' luggage? (I wonder . . .)
   I wonder if airlines will ever stop losing passengers' luggage.
2. How do I correct a mistake on my phone bill? (I'd like to know . . .)
3. Why can't I use my cell phone in an elevator? (The thing I don't get is . . .)
4. How can I get tickets to sold-out concerts? (I want to find out . . .)
5. When will the government deal with global warming? (I'd like to know . . .)
6. Why do people complain so much? (. . . is something I can't understand.)

4 VOCABULARY & SPEAKING

I'm totally baffled!

A Look at these words that describe feelings. Put them in the correct columns.

| annoyed | confused | depressed | enraged | humiliated | insulted | mystified | stunned |
| baffled | demoralized | discouraged | frustrated | infuriated | irritated | saddened | |

Confused feelings	Angry feelings	Sad feelings
baffled	annoyed	

B **Pair work** Complete the sentences with your own information. Then discuss your answers with a partner.

1. I'm totally baffled by . . .
2. I get so infuriated when . . .
3. I always get discouraged when . . .
4. I wouldn't be demoralized even if . . .
5. I remember feeling stunned when . . .
6. I would feel insulted if . . .

"I'm totally baffled by people who can speak a lot of languages. How do they remember so many different words and grammar rules?"

VOCABULARY PLUS see page 139

LESSON B   Let's do something about it!

5 DISCUSSION
A word to the wise

A **Pair work** Read the advice about how to avoid consumer problems. Can you add any more ideas to the list?

Buyer Beware!
SMART ADVICE FOR SMART SHOPPERS

- Buy from a reputable company.
- Make sure there's a guarantee.
- Examine your purchases before you buy.
- Do some comparison shopping.
- Find out about the return policy.
- Find out how the item should be cared for.

B **Group work** Discuss a time when you had a problem with something you bought. Would the advice in part A have helped you?

"I bought some really expensive luggage last month, and I was enraged when, after just a week, one of the wheels came off."
"Oh, you're kidding. Did you take it back to the store?"
"Yes, but they told me I couldn't return it because I'd bought it on sale. I should have asked about their return policy . . ."

Useful expressions

Sympathizing
Oh, you're kidding.
That's ridiculous.
What a pain.

6 ROLE PLAY
I'd like to return this.

A Read the store returns policy in part B. Is there a similar policy at the stores where you shop?

B **Pair work** Take turns role-playing a customer and a clerk at a returns counter. Use the returns policy and the situations below.

STORE RETURNS POLICY: All items must be in good condition and accompanied by a receipt. No cash refunds; store credit only. No items returned after two weeks unless under warranty. No return of items purchased on sale or with coupons.

Situation 1
- T-shirt
- have receipt
- shrank after washing
- now too small

Situation 2
- laptop
- receipt at home
- defective
- still under warranty

Situation 3
- camera
- lost receipt
- not very user-friendly
- want to exchange

"I'd like to return this T-shirt, please. I can't understand why it shrank after I washed it."
"I wonder whether you followed the washing instructions properly."
"I certainly did!"
"That's fine, then. May I see your receipt, please?"

UNIT 10 The art of complaining

7 READING
The power of one voice

A Pair work What steps would you take if someone damaged one of your valuable possessions? Discuss with a partner. Then read the article and find out what Dave Caroll did. Did he take any of the steps you discussed?

Dave Carroll Airs a Complaint

Dave Carroll was ready to quit his 20-year career as an independent musician. Then, an airline broke his guitar and changed his life.

The airline wouldn't budge on Dave's request for $1,200 in flight vouchers to cover repairs to his $3,500 Taylor guitar. When he got "The Final No!" email after nine months of negotiations, he wrote back to say he wasn't without options.

Dave said that if he were a lawyer, he might have sued the airline, but as a songwriter, he had other tools at his disposal. He vowed to write two or three songs, make a music video for each one, and post them on YouTube.

"After months of feeling frustrated and angry about the ordeal, for the first time I felt empowered, as though a weight had been lifted from me. I changed gears from someone who *wanted* something to someone who was going to *do* something."

His goal was to reach one million views in the next year. Four days after he posted the first video, he hit a million views. The airline called him a day after the video was released to offer the same $1,200 in flight vouchers he'd asked for previously, plus an extra $1,200 in cash. Carroll refused the offer. His goal had moved beyond compensation to sharing his story and improving conditions for all travelers.

His newfound fame has revived his music career. His trilogy of songs about his experience has had approximately 15 million YouTube views. He's done media interviews and given speeches around the world. Ironically, the airline now uses his videos to train staff and pays him a license fee to do so, at his request.

He's also helped launch a website, Gripevine.com, for people to air problems and get them fixed. Companies now know that a disgruntled customer's view can go viral in a heartbeat and reach an immense audience. As Dave tells businesses, it's vital for companies to listen and learn.

Source: "Dave Carroll is still having problems with airlines," by Ellen Roseman, *The Toronto Star*

B Pair work Number the events in the correct order. Write *X* for the two events that are not part of Dave's story. Then take turns telling the story in your own words.

____ a. Dave decided to use his songwriting skills to address his problem in a creative way.
____ b. Dave rejected the airline's offer even though they'd doubled his original request.
____ c. Dave sued the airline for the amount of money it would cost to repair his guitar.
____ d. Dave's guitar was damaged by an airline, and they refused to compensate him.
____ e. The airline offered Dave what he wanted after he posted his song on YouTube.
____ f. Dave gave up on his dreams of becoming a musician after 20 years in the business.
____ g. Dave helped start an online consumer group and relaunched his career.

C Group work Discuss these questions. Then share your answers with the class.

1. What made Dave finally feel empowered during his struggle with the airline?
2. In what ways has social media given ordinary people more power? Give examples.

LESSON B Let's do something about it!

11 VALUES
LESSON A ▶ How honest are you?

1 STARTING POINT
What would you do?

A Look at the situations and people's responses. What would you do?

If you accidentally damaged a parked car in a parking lot . . .

"If the owner weren't around, I'd leave a note with my phone number."

"I wouldn't leave a note if the owner weren't around."

If you found out your co-worker got the job using false credentials . . .

"I would keep it a secret only if I liked my co-worker."

"I would keep it a secret unless my boss asked me directly about it."

If you found some money on the street . . .

"I wouldn't try to return it unless it were a large amount."

"Even if I were really broke, I'd give the money to the police."

B Pair work Now read these statistics. Do you find them surprising? Why or why not?

Of the people surveyed . . .

62% would never fail to report damaging a parked car even if nobody were present.

48% think it is unacceptable to use false credentials on a job application.

18% wouldn't keep money they found on the street.

58% would never illegally avoid paying the fare on public transportation.

25% think it's never OK to exceed the speed limit while driving.

Source: British Election Study at the University of Essex, Economic and Social Research Council

2 LISTENING
Finders keepers

Listen to Aaron and Leanne talking about finding something. Are these statements true or false, or does the person not say? Choose the correct answer.

	True	False	Doesn't say
1. Aaron's son wanted to keep the wallet and spend the money.	☐	☐	☐
2. Aaron's son received a thank-you card as a reward.	☐	☐	☐
3. The owner of the book probably didn't care much about it.	☐	☐	☐
4. Leanne will probably return the book.	☐	☐	☐

3 GRAMMAR

Present unreal conditional with *unless, only if,* and *even if*

Unless clauses include exceptions that would change the speaker's decision.
I **wouldn't** try to return it **unless** it **were** a large amount.
I **would** keep it a secret **unless** my boss **asked** me directly about it.

Only if clauses stress the condition for the result.
I **would** keep it a secret **only if** I **liked** my co-worker.

Even if clauses are followed by unexpected results.
Even if I **were** really broke, **I'd** give the money to the police.

GRAMMAR PLUS see page 126

A Look at the Starting Point on page 88 again. Look at the responses to the first situation. Are they different in meaning? If so, how?

B Choose the words that are true for you. Then complete the sentences.

1. If a cashier undercharged me, I (would) / wouldn't tell him if / (even if) . . .
   If a cashier undercharged me, I would tell him even if it were a small difference.
2. I *would / wouldn't* borrow a lot of money from a friend *only if / unless* . . .
3. I *would / wouldn't* return a gift I'd received to the store *if / unless* . . .
4. I *would / wouldn't* "temporarily borrow" an unlocked bicycle on the street *only if / even if* . . .
5. I *would / wouldn't* report my friend for skipping work *only if / unless* . . .

4 VOCABULARY & SPEAKING

It's a little unethical.

A These words describe people's ethics and attitudes. Which prefixes give them the opposite meaning? Put the words in the correct columns.

| acceptable | approving | fair | legal | rational | scrupulous |
| agreeable | ethical | honest | logical | responsible | trustworthy |

dis-	il-	ir-	un-
			unacceptable

B Pair work Use the vocabulary words in part A to discuss these questions.

1. Would you ever make an international call from work to save money?
2. Would you ever play a practical joke on your friends?
3. Would you ever tell a friend with a terrible new haircut that you think it's fantastic?

VOCABULARY PLUS see page 140

LESSON A How honest are you?

5 DISCUSSION
Ethical dilemmas

A Read these situations. What would you do?

What Would You Do?

1 You've had plans for several weeks to visit your aunt. The day before, your friend invites you to a really great party the same night.
- Would you cancel your original plans?
- If so, would you tell the truth or "a white lie" about why you were canceling?
- Would you cancel your plans even if you knew your aunt were looking forward to seeing you?

2 You're at a convenience store, and you see someone shoplifting a can of soup.
- Would you tell the clerk?
- What if the shoplifter were a woman with a small child?
- Would it make a difference if the shoplifter looked dangerous?

3 You work full-time during the day. You're also a part-time student in an evening course, so you have a student ID card. Businesses all over town give discounts to students.
- Would you use your student ID to get the cheaper prices?
- What if you earned a high salary at your job?
- Would it make a difference if you were buying from a major chain store or from a small mom-and-pop business?

B **Group work** Share your answers and give reasons for each. Then agree on the best course of action for each situation.

"Unless it were a special occasion for my aunt, I might leave a little early so I could get to the party before it ended."

6 DISCUSSION
Too good to be true

A Which of these situations seem reliable? Choose those that seem legitimate.

☐ 1. A website offers free international phone service.
☐ 2. A company sends you an email asking you to confirm your credit card details online.
☐ 3. Someone on the street asks you to sign a petition that requires your address and phone number.
☐ 4. A television ad offers a set of knives worth $300 for just $75.

B **Pair work** Discuss these or similar situations. Share your own experiences or those of people you know.

"I once bought a kitchen appliance that I saw advertised on TV. The price was really good, and it worked well at first, but after a few weeks, it broke."

7 WRITING
Thesis statements

> A topic sentence states the main idea of a single paragraph. A thesis statement introduces the topic of a composition. It is often located at the beginning or end of the first paragraph.

A Read the composition and choose the best thesis statement from the choices below. Then, write a *T* where you think the thesis statement should appear.

1. I've made some bad decisions.
2. We learn a lot from the decisions we make.
3. I have good and bad memories of old friendships.

When I'm faced with a decision that puts my ethics on the line, I think about what similar situations in the past have taught me. In my life, I've made both good and bad choices.

One of my good decisions resulted in a casual friend becoming a very close friend. A college classmate gave me a lottery ticket for my birthday. As she gave it to me, she joked that if I won, I should split the prize with her. I ended up winning $500. At the time, I was saving for a new tablet, and with the $500, I had enough money. I considered not telling my friend that I'd won. But I felt dishonest and disloyal, and I gave her half. I'll always be glad I did, and I wouldn't do it any differently today, even if I really needed all the money. Today, she is still one of my best friends.

One of my bad decisions ruined a friendship. A former classmate wanted a job with my company and asked me to recommend her. I knew she didn't have very good work habits. I told her I would do it only if she promised to work hard. She was hired, but three months later, she was fired because my boss thought she was irresponsible and her work was unacceptable. I was fairly new at the company myself, and my company is still a little unsure about trusting my judgment now. I don't have much to do with her these days.

I believe that good and bad decisions are a part of everyone's personal development. Is it possible to learn from those experiences? I think it is because even the bad ones help to prepare you for the future.

B Write a four-paragraph composition about a happy memory or a regret. Follow these guidelines.

1st paragraph: Introduce your topic in the paragraph. Begin or end the paragraph with your thesis statement.

2nd paragraph: Write about a decision you would make again.

3rd paragraph: Write about a decision you would make differently.

4th paragraph: End with a strong conclusion.

Your thesis statement . . .
- should contain *a single idea*.
- should be neither too *general* nor too *specific*.
- should unify *all the paragraphs*.
- can be *improved* as you write.

C Group work Take turns reading your compositions. Is the thesis statement too general? Does it need to be improved?

LESSON B ▶ Taking stock

1 STARTING POINT
I wish . . .

A Read these messages. Match each message with one of the values below.

a. careful spending
c. perseverance
e. career advancement
b. concern for others
d. good family relations
f. good cross-cultural relations

The Connected World

Today's questions: I've had so many cool friends in my life. I wish I'd stayed in touch with all of them! Is there anything you wish you'd done differently? What do you wish you could change right now?

____ **1. Mika22** — I wish I had enough nerve to ask for a promotion. I like my job, but I've been in the same position for several years. If only my boss would consider promoting me!

____ **2. Ivan007** — I love and respect my mother and father a lot. I wish I hadn't given them such a hard time when I was growing up. I'm just happy they forgave me for all those rough times.

____ **3. Wishful** — I'm ashamed of all the money I've wasted. If only I'd saved more over the last few years. Now I want to rent my own apartment, and I can't afford to! Starting today, I'm going to stop buying things I don't need.

____ **4. JackD** — I used to travel to Mexico for my job about once a month. I probably would have been more successful if I had spoken more Spanish. I wish I'd taken a few Spanish classes.

____ **5. SportsFan** — When I was a kid, I tried lots of things – sports, languages, music – and I enjoyed them all, but I always lost interest after a while. If I had stuck with something, I could have gotten good at it.

____ **6. Ruby65** — I wish I could find the time to do volunteer work. I feel I'm not contributing enough to the community. Maybe I can find time to volunteer at the hospital in my neighborhood.

B **Pair work** Which person in part A are you most like? Which of the values are the most important? What are some of the values you learned when you were growing up?

"I'm similar to Ruby65. I really think it's important to show concern for other people. As I was growing up, my parents also taught me the importance of . . ."

2 GRAMMAR
Wishes and regrets

For wishes about the present and future, use *wish* + simple past, past continuous, or *could* / *would* + verb.
I **wish** I **had** enough nerve to ask for a promotion.
I **wish** I **could find** the time to do volunteer work.

For regrets about the past, use *wish* + past perfect.
I **wish** I**'d taken** a few Spanish classes.
I **wish** I **hadn't given** my parents such a hard time when I was growing up.

For regrets about the past, use *if* + past perfect and *could* / *would have* + past participle.
If I **had stuck** with something, I **could have gotten** good at it.

For strong wishes about the present or future, or for strong regrets about the past, use *if only*.
***If only* clauses are often used without a main clause.**
If only my boss **would consider** promoting me!

GRAMMAR PLUS see page 127

A Look at the Starting Point on page 92 again. Which sentences express regrets about the past? Which ones describe wishes for the present or future?

B Rewrite these statements using the words in parentheses. Compare answers with a partner. Are any of the sentences true for you?

1. I can't find the time to exercise. (I wish . . .)
   I wish I could find the time to exercise.
2. My grades weren't very good last semester. (If only . . .)
3. I don't know how to dance very well. (I wish . . .)
4. I didn't apply for that interesting job at work. (I wish . . .)
5. I'm feeling very stressed these days. (I wish . . .)
6. I never learned how to swim when I was a child. (If only . . .)
7. I gave away my old guitar last year. (If only . . .)
8. I watched too much TV and didn't read enough when I was a kid. (If only . . .)

C Complete these sentences with your own wishes or regrets and add extra information. Then compare answers with a partner.

1. If only I had enough money to . . . ! Then I wouldn't . . .
   If only I had enough money to buy a motorcycle!
   Then I wouldn't have to take the bus to class.
2. I wish I could find the time to . . . . If I could, I would . . .
3. I wish I had learned how to . . . when I was a kid. If I had, I'd . . .
4. If only I knew how to . . . . Then I could . . .
5. I wish my friends would . . . so that . . .
6. If only I had listened to my parents when they told me . . . because . . .
7. I wish they would pass a law that says . . . . If they did, . . .
8. If only I had the courage to . . . . Then I would . . .

LESSON B Taking stock 93

3 VOCABULARY & SPEAKING
Personal values

A What words describe people's values? Complete the chart with the correct noun or adjective.

Noun	Adjective	Noun	Adjective	Noun	Adjective
compassion	*compassionate*		indifferent	selfishness	
	discreet	kindness		sensitivity	
generosity		resilience			tender
	honest		respectful		tolerant

B Pair work Which three values do you think are most important? Decide with a partner. Give your reasons.

"We thought generosity, tolerance, and honesty were most important. Generosity is an important value because if you help people, they might help you one day. Tolerance matters because . . ."

VOCABULARY PLUS see page 140

4 LISTENING & SPEAKING
Three important values

🔊 **A** Listen to these on-the-street interviews. What values do these people think are important? Number the values in the order you hear them.

___ honesty   ___ privacy   ___ respect

🔊 **B** Listen again. Whose answer did you agree with the most? Why do you think so?

"I'd say I agreed with the first woman the most. If you're not honest, you'll only get yourself into trouble. Plus, telling the truth is the right thing to do."

5 SPEAKING
Grant me a wish.

A If you could have three wishes, what would they be? Make a list.

B Pair work Compare your wishes with a partner. Then share your answers with the class.

"My first wish would be for my family to stay healthy and happy. Second, I would wish for more peace in the world. For my last wish, . . ."

6 READING
Subway Superman

A **Pair work** Read the title and the first paragraph of the news article. What would you have done if you were Wesley Autrey? Discuss, and then read the article.

NEW YORK HONORS A HERO

It started as a typical day for Wesley Autrey, a 50-year-old construction worker in New York City. It was about 12:45 P.M., and he was waiting on a subway platform to take his daughters home before he went to work. He suddenly noticed a man nearby have convulsions and collapse. Mr. Autrey and two women went to help the stranger. The man, Cameron Hollopeter, managed to get to his feet, but then stumbled at the edge of the platform and fell onto the subway tracks. Mr. Autrey looked up and saw the lights of the subway train approaching through the tunnel.

What would you do? Stand horrified and watch helplessly? Most people would jump in to help, but only if there were no train in sight. Mr. Autrey acted quickly. He leapt down onto the track. He realized that he didn't have time to get Mr. Hollopeter and himself back up on the platform before the train arrived, so he lay on top of the man and pressed down as hard as he could. Although the driver tried to stop the train before it reached them, he couldn't. Five cars passed over them before the train finally stopped. The cars had passed only inches from his head. His first words were to ask the onlookers to tell his daughters he was OK.

New York loves a hero. And there was no question that Mr. Autrey's actions had been just that – heroic. He became an overnight sensation. People couldn't get enough of the story. The media named him the "Subway Superman." New York City Mayor Michael Bloomberg gave him the Bronze Medallion, the city's highest honor. (In the past, this honor has gone to such people as General Douglas MacArthur, Martin Luther King Jr., and Muhammad Ali.) Mr. Autrey was also asked to appear on several high-profile television talk shows.

His selfless bravery was also rewarded with money and gifts. Among other things, Mr. Autrey received: $10,000 from Donald Trump, a $5,000 gift card from the Gap clothing store, a new Jeep, tickets and backstage passes to a Beyoncé concert, and a free one-year public transit pass. A "Disney ambassador" thanked him with a one-week all-expenses-paid trip to Disney World and tickets to see *The Lion King* on Broadway.

How did Autrey, a Navy veteran, react to all this? Honorably. He said, "I don't feel like I did anything spectacular; I just saw someone who needed help. I did what I felt was right."

B Read the article again. Are these statements true or false? Choose the correct answer. Correct the false statements.

	True	False
1. Autrey hadn't noticed Hollopeter before he fell onto the tracks.	☐	☐
2. There was very little space between Autrey and the bottom of the train.	☐	☐
3. Autrey jumped onto the tracks because he wanted to be a hero.	☐	☐

C **Group work** Discuss these questions.

1. Have you ever had the opportunity to help someone in trouble or in danger?
2. Why do you think so many businesses wanted to reward Mr. Autrey?

12 MOVING AROUND
LESSON A ▶ Culture shock

1 STARTING POINT
The benefits of studying abroad

A Read this website. Choose three benefits of studying a language abroad that you feel are the most important.

LTI LANGUAGE TRAVELERS INSTITUTE

OPENING DOORS TO THE WORLD
Study Abroad with Language Travelers Institute!

- LTI SCHOOLS
- STUDY ABROAD
- CONTACT US

Consider enrolling in one of LTI's affordable programs of language study abroad. Then imagine yourself by the end of next year:
- You will have been studying your chosen language for 12 months.
- You will have been interacting with people from other cultures, which will have changed the way you view the world.
- You will have been living in a fascinating foreign land.

And, if you're like over 90% of LTI's former students, by this time next year:
- Your self-confidence will have increased.
- Your commitment to language study will have gotten stronger.
- You will have made many fascinating new friends!

Study abroad with Language Travelers Institute and the world will become your oyster.

B Pair work Discuss your choices. What are some other benefits of studying or living abroad?

"I think interacting with people from other cultures is the most important benefit."

2 VOCABULARY & SPEAKING
Words of encouragement

A Complete these verbs and phrases with a preposition from the box.

| about | in | of | to | with |

1. adjust _to_
2. be excited _____
3. be scared _____
4. be familiar _____
5. become aware _____
6. get accustomed _____
7. look forward _____
8. participate _____
9. take advantage _____

B Pair work What challenges do people face when they live or study abroad? Discuss with a partner using the verbs and phrases in part A.

"Sometimes people are scared of starting a new job abroad because they aren't familiar with the routines."

VOCABULARY PLUS see page 141

3 GRAMMAR

Future perfect and future perfect continuous

Use the future perfect to emphasize that something will be completed or achieved by a particular point in the future.
By this time next year, your self-confidence **will have increased**.

Use the future perfect continuous to emphasize the duration of an activity in progress at a particular point in the future.
By the end of next year, you **will have been studying** your chosen language for 12 months.

GRAMMAR PLUS see page 128

A Look at the Starting Point on page 96 again. Can you find more examples of the future perfect and the future perfect continuous?

B These sentences about Joon's year abroad all have mistakes. Correct the mistakes using the future with *will*, the future perfect, or the future perfect continuous. Then compare answers with a partner.

1. By this time tomorrow, Joon ~~will travel~~ *will have been traveling* for 24 hours.

2. By the end of next week, he will have been receiving his student ID card and registered for classes.

3. He'll be going out more after a few weeks because he will have been more familiar with the city.

4. After studying English for a few months, he will have felt more confident about speaking to people.

5. By this time next year, his younger sister will have been visiting him once or twice. When she's older, she probably will have wanted to study abroad, too.

6. I'm sure he will change a lot by the time he comes back to Korea.

7. His family will have been surprised when he gets back because he will have been changing so much.

8. And just think – the next time we see him, Joon will turn 22 already, and he will be away for a year!

C Use these time expressions to write sentences using the future perfect or future perfect continuous. Then share them with a partner.

1. Before this class ends, . . .
2. By the end of the day, . . .
3. By the end of the week, . . .
4. At the end of the year, . . .
5. In two years' time, . . .
6. By the year 2030, . . .

LESSON A Culture shock

4 DISCUSSION
Customs and traditions

A Read this list of Canadian customs. Are they the same as or different from those where you live? Choose the correct answer.

		Same	Different
01	Both men and women shake hands with each other when they meet.	☐	☐
02	Business meetings are friendly, but there isn't much socializing beforehand.	☐	☐
03	Lunch is usually a fairly light meal that doesn't last long.	☐	☐
04	People are usually punctual for business appointments.	☐	☐
05	It's common to ask people you meet what kind of work they do.	☐	☐
06	Many people eat dinner early in the evening, around 6:00 P.M.	☐	☐
07	At the dinner table, the fork is generally held in the left hand and the knife in the right.	☐	☐
08	People offer to take their shoes off when entering somebody's home.	☐	☐
09	When invited to someone's home, a gift, such as flowers or dessert, is usually expected.	☐	☐
10	Most people open gifts as soon as they receive them.	☐	☐

B **Group work** How do you feel about the customs in part A? Explain your opinions.

"I think women should kiss on the cheek when they meet. Just shaking hands seems kind of cold somehow."

5 LISTENING
When in Rome . . .

A Listen to Andrew, Rachel, and Layla talking about their experiences abroad. Answer the questions.

1. What helped each of them get used to their new living situation?
2. What did each person find difficult to adjust to?

B Listen again. Did Andrew (*A*), Rachel (*R*), or Layla (*L*) do these things? Write the correct letter.

____ 1. felt homesick
____ 2. had fun playing a sport
____ 3. enjoyed food with friends
____ 4. didn't feel connected to others at first
____ 5. ate dinner late at night
____ 6. thought people talked about themselves too much
____ 7. enjoyed the old buildings
____ 8. watched comedy shows on TV
____ 9. tried to talk about herself

6 WRITING
Conclusions

> The conclusion can close your composition by restating the main idea, summarizing the main points, looking to the future, making recommendations, or a combination of these methods.

A Read these two concluding paragraphs. Which methods do the writers use? Underline the parts of the conclusions that helped you decide.

Overall, for the majority of young people, taking a year off to travel has not replaced the traditional postsecondary pursuit of higher education. For most high school graduates, studying or training for a career will remain the most likely path. However, there are still many young people who save as much money as they can in order to see foreign sights and experience foreign cultures. Taking time to travel may put them behind a year as far as college and careers are concerned, but they say the personal growth is worth it.

In brief, there are real benefits to studying abroad. While it is certainly possible to learn the language in a country where it is not widely spoken, living abroad offers limitless possibilities for improvement. Additionally, foreign students have a real opportunity to hone their life skills. Generally, they are responsible for everything from money management, accommodations, and meals to ensuring that they have a good balance between their social life and school life. Studying abroad offers not only language lessons, but also life lessons, and is well worth considering.

B Find these linking words or phrases in the conclusions. How are they used? Do you know any others that have similar meanings?

| additionally | generally | however | in brief | overall |

C Write a composition about living or traveling abroad. Choose one of these topics or one of your own. Your conclusion should use at least one of the methods described and some linking words or phrases.

- culture shock
- group travel
- independent travel
- studying abroad

D **Pair work** Exchange papers with a partner and answer these questions.

1. What methods did your partner use in his or her conclusion?
2. Are the linking words used effectively? Why or why not?
3. Can you offer any suggestions to improve your partner's conclusion?

LESSON A Culture shock

LESSON B ▶ Traveler or tourist?

1 STARTING POINT
Travel tips

A Read these people's experiences and the expert's advice. Can you think of any other advice?

TERRY'S Travel Tips

Get advice from Terry Tripper, the travel expert, and share your own travel tips.

Meg B. says: A woman fell down in front of me during a sightseeing tour. I helped her up, but soon after, I couldn't find my wallet. Do you think she might have taken it?

Terry says: It's very likely. If you hadn't been so nice, you would probably still have your wallet. It's a common scam – someone pretends to be in trouble, but actually turns out to be a thief!

Bruno H. says: I want to share a tip my friend gave me that I used on my last vacation. If you're worried about losing your passport, like I am, don't carry it around with you. Just keep it in your hotel room.

Terry says: That is a good tip if there is a safe in your room. If not, keep your passport with you at all times. If someone had broken into your room, you would probably still be trying to get home!

Kim N. says: On my last trip abroad, I brought a little notebook and pen to help me communicate while shopping. If I couldn't find something, I'd draw a picture. If I hadn't had that notebook and pen, my friends wouldn't be thanking me for the awesome souvenirs I brought them!

Terry says: That's a great idea! When phrasebooks and dictionaries don't help, a picture can be worth a thousand words. But you know there are also some great apps for that, right? Check out this website.

B Pair work What travel questions would you ask Terry? Tell your partner. Then try to offer advice to each other.

"I want to buy souvenirs from the places I'm going to visit, but I also like to travel light. Should I store them at the airport or somewhere else?"

"The best thing would be to mail them home. If you don't mind waiting, use surface mail instead of airmail. It's cheaper."

2 LISTENING
Things went wrong.

A Listen to Cindy and Scott talking about their travel problems. What happened to each person?

B Listen again. Choose the statements you think are probably true. Compare your answers with a partner. Give reasons.

☐ 1. Cindy has a unique, easy-to-see name tag on her luggage.
☐ 2. Cindy travels frequently.
☐ 3. Scott likes peace and quiet when he travels.
☐ 4. Scott slept soundly all the way to Panama City.

3 GRAMMAR

Mixed conditionals

Use *had / hadn't* + past participle and *would / wouldn't* to talk about hypothetical events in the past that have effects on the present.

If you **hadn't been** so nice, you **would** probably still **have** your wallet!
If someone **had broken into** your room, you **would** probably still **be trying** to get home!

GRAMMAR PLUS see page 129

A Look at the Starting Point on page 100 again. Find another mixed conditional sentence. Does this sentence describe actual or hypothetical events?

B Complete these sentences with the correct form of the verbs in parentheses.

1. If I _____**had been**_____ (be) more adventurous when I was younger, I _____**wouldn't have**_____ (not have) any regrets about the things I missed.

2. The airline lost my luggage. If I _____ (bring) a change of clothes in my carry-on bag, I _____ (not shop) for new clothes now.

3. This flight is so long! If I _____ (not buy) an economy ticket, I _____ (be) more comfortable now.

4. If you _____ (learn) to speak some Mandarin before moving to Taipei, you _____ (be able to) ask someone for directions now.

5. If Martha _____ (not become) a flight attendant, she probably _____ (not travel) as much as she does.

4 DISCUSSION

Your own trip

A Pair work Have you ever had problems on vacation? Tell your partner. Use the topics below or your own ideas.

- health
- accommodations
- food
- safety
- language
- getting around
- costs
- weather

"I went to the beach last week, but the weather was awful."
"Why? Was it rainy?"
"No, it was too sunny. If it hadn't been so sunny, I wouldn't have this terrible sunburn now."

B Group work Share your bad travel experiences. Get advice about what you could have done differently.

LESSON B   Traveler or tourist?

5 VOCABULARY
One word or two?

A Combine the items from the boxes to make compound adjectives.

culturally	assured	hearted	motivated
non	aware	judgmental	reliant
open	conforming	minded	sensitive
self			

culturally aware, nonjudgmental, open-minded, . . .

B **Pair work** Are the characteristics in part A important when you travel? Give an example for each one.

"If you're culturally aware, you'll find it easier to accept cultural differences."

VOCABULARY PLUS see page 141

6 ROLE PLAY
Planning a trip

A **Group work** Imagine you are planning a vacation. Discuss these questions. Write notes about what your group decides for each question.

1. Where would you like to go?
2. How long would you like your stay to last?
3. Would you like to go with a tour group or on your own?
4. What type of accommodations do you prefer?
5. What kinds of activities would you like to do during the day?
6. What sorts of evening activities would you prefer?
7. What would each person's budget be?
8. What types of transportation would you plan on using?

B **Class activity** Choose someone in your group to act as a travel agent and present your vacation to the class. The class votes on the best itinerary.

"We have planned a truly exotic vacation for you in the remote Galápagos Islands! You'll stay for seven unforgettable days in a five-star resort . . ."

7 READING
Solo travel

A What are the best ways to experience a new place when you travel? Make a list. Then read the article to compare your list with the author's.

Get Yourself LOST

Travelers to a new city are often encouraged to take a bus tour. The thinking is that they can later return to the places that **captivated** them, but that's nonsense! What you see from the inside of a fast-moving bus is sanitized and unreal, utterly removed from the authentic sights, sounds, and smells outside.

The best way to experience any destination is by foot, without an itinerary, wandering where your spirit leads you. Even in the largest cities, the **savvy** traveler **plunges** into the very center of town and walks down the nearest street, experiencing the actual life of the people while looking into the grocery stores and courtyards. You eventually get to many of the same sites that are on the bus route – the museums, the monuments, the city hall – but you will have witnessed so much more because you will have felt the contemporary life of the city you're visiting.

"But what if I get lost?" people ask. No one ever gets permanently lost in a major city. Eventually, a trolley or bus passes with the words "Central Station" on its front and you can easily return to the center of town. Besides, the most wonderful things can happen if you do get lost, such as stopping at a sidewalk café to sit and relax and then asking directions from the locals at the next table. Hopefully, your trip may be **enhanced** by this encounter. Here are a few ways to make the most of your travels:

> **KNOW BEFORE YOU GO.** Before you depart, spend time learning about the history and culture of your destination so you will better understand the place you're visiting.

> **MOVE AROUND LIKE A LOCAL.** Use the local subways, trams, and buses. You'll not only save money, you'll learn how people live there, and you'll gain a realistic perspective of the city.

> **CHECK THE BULLETIN BOARDS.** Bulletin boards list free lectures, concerts, workshops, and social gatherings, giving you a chance to join or meet the area's most **dynamic** residents.

> **TAKE A WALKING TOUR.** If you must book a guided tour, select the nonstandard, inexpensive kinds conducted on foot.

So, the next time you feel lured by a sightseeing bus tour, save your money and instead, wander around on your own. I promise you a time you'll remember fondly.

Source: "Get Yourself Lost," by Arthur Frommer

B Find the boldfaced words in the article. Then choose the correct words to complete the sentences.

1. If something **captivates** you, you're *upset / captured / delighted* by it.
2. A **savvy** traveler is *refined / experienced / adventurous*.
3. When you **plunge** into an activity, you probably *walk away from it / throw yourself into it / stumble into it*.
4. If you **enhance** your reading skills, you *upgrade / restore / prolong* them.
5. **Dynamic** people are more *cautious / unstable / interesting* than others.

C Pair work How do your travel habits compare with those in the article? Which ideas do you think you'll try the next time you visit a new city? Why?

COMMUNICATION REVIEW
UNITS 10–12

✓ SELF-ASSESSMENT

How well can you do these things? Choose the best answer.

I can . . .	Very well	OK	A little
▶ Describe annoying behavior (Ex. 1)	☐	☐	☐
▶ Make and respond to customer complaints (Ex. 1)	☐	☐	☐
▶ Discuss hypothetical situations in my present and future life (Ex. 2)	☐	☐	☐
▶ Understand the main points of a training workshop about customer service (Ex. 3)	☐	☐	☐
▶ Express and explain my opinions in a discussion about living and working in a different culture (Ex. 4)	☐	☐	☐
▶ Make hypotheses about past and present events in my life (Ex. 5)	☐	☐	☐

Now do the corresponding exercises. Was your assessment correct?

1 ROLE PLAY
Annoying customers

A What do you think annoys these people about their passengers or customers?

1. bus drivers
2. flight attendants
3. tech support workers
4. waiters/waitresses

"Something that probably makes bus drivers crazy is when people complain that the buses are running late. It usually isn't the drivers' fault."

B Pair work Take turns playing the role of a customer complaining and an employee responding to the complaints.

2 DISCUSSION
I'd like to try . . .

A Look at these questions and write answers that are true for you.

1. What is something you'd like to try, even if it were a little risky?
2. What is something you would do only if it were a matter of life or death?
3. Where is someplace you wouldn't want to go unless someone went with you?

B Pair work Discuss your answers with a partner.

"I'd like to try scuba diving at night, even if it were a little risky. I think diving in the ocean at night must be incredible."

3 LISTENING
Training

A Listen to a training workshop. What job are the trainees going to do?

B Listen again. Are these statements true or false? Choose the correct answer.

	True	False
1. Sammy would try to get the customer on a flight the same day.	☐	☐
2. Andrea says the customer should have left more time between flights.	☐	☐
3. Ricardo says the customer should be ashamed for being late.	☐	☐
4. Hannah would direct the customer to a place where she could get refreshed.	☐	☐

4 DISCUSSION
Culture shock

A **Pair work** How important are these personality traits for someone who is living and working in a new culture? Number them from 1 to 6 (1 = most important, 6 = least important).

It's important to be . . .

- ☐ culturally aware
- ☐ nonjudgmental
- ☐ open-minded
- ☐ self-assured
- ☐ self-aware
- ☐ self-reliant

B **Group work** Join another pair. Explain your rankings to the group and discuss any differences of opinion.

5 DISCUSSION
What if . . . ?

A **Pair work** Discuss the questions.

How would your life be different today if . . .

1. you'd been born in another country?
2. you'd grown up in a much smaller or larger family?
3. you hadn't learned any English?
4. you hadn't met your best friend?

B **Group work** What event or circumstance has had the biggest effect on you? How would your life be different if that event hadn't happened?

"I think growing up in an extended family had the biggest effect on me. If my grandmother hadn't been living with us, I wouldn't have such an awareness of my culture and my ancestors."

GRAMMAR PLUS

7A Passive of present continuous, present perfect, future

> If the agent (the person or thing doing the action) is unknown or obvious from the context, it's better to use a passive form. However, if the person or thing doing the action needs to be emphasized, it's better to use an active form.
> The spyware **is being used** to collect information about college students. *(Agent is unknown.)*
> Social networking sites **have been used** in criminal investigations. *(Agent is clear from context.)*
> A criminal organization **has created** this virus, not an amateur hacker. *(Agent is emphasized.)*
>
> **The passive is very rarely used with the present perfect continuous. Use the passive of the present perfect instead.**
> People **have been posting** more videos to the Internet this year than ever before.
> More videos **have been posted** to the Internet this year than ever before.

1 For each pair of sentences, is it better to use the passive or active form? Choose *a* or *b*.

1. ☑ a. More U.S. employers will likely allow access to social networking sites.
   ☐ b. Access to social networking sites will likely be allowed.

2. ☐ a. Soon, inventors will invent smartphones that don't require a battery.
   ☐ b. Smartphones that don't require a battery will be invented soon.

3. ☐ a. Most cell phone companies are now offering unlimited-use plans.
   ☐ b. Unlimited-use plans are being offered now.

4. ☐ a. Teachers might be teaching more high school students with educational computer games.
   ☐ b. More high school students might be taught with educational computer games.

2 Complete the sentences with the correct active or passive form of the verb in parentheses.

1. Recently, social networking sites _have become_ (become) popular with all age groups.
2. Every week, free software _____ (download) on computers everywhere.
3. In the years to come, podcasts _____ (use) more often in educational programs.
4. Lately, children _____ (ask) for cell phones at a younger and younger age.
5. More sophisticated viruses _____ (create) all the time.
6. For years, hackers _____ (try) to use spyware to commit identity theft.
7. In years to come, more and more data _____ (store) in the cloud.
8. I recently discovered that my neighbors _____ (use) my Wi-Fi many times.
9. In the next decade, more job interviews _____ (hold) online.
10. Since I last visited this blog, several older posts _____ (remove).

7B Negative and tag questions for giving opinions

> Use past negative and tag questions to offer an opinion about a past event and invite someone to react.
> **Wasn't it** weird how the manager's microphone kept turning on and off during his speech?
> **Didn't it seem** like the manager's speech would never end?
> **Shouldn't the company have provided** us with coffee before the speech?
> The manager's speech was really boring, **wasn't it**?
> The manager has given some pretty boring speeches, **hasn't he**?
> The manager's speech had just put about everyone to sleep when the fire alarm rang, **hadn't it**?
>
> In informal spoken English, *they* can be used as the pronoun in tag questions when the subject is *somebody*, *someone*, *everybody*, *everyone*, *nobody*, or *no one*.
> **Everyone** we know had a cell phone in school, didn't **they**?   Yes, they did.
> **Somebody** has hacked into your computer, haven't **they**?   Yes, they have. / No, they haven't.
>
> Use an affirmative tag question when the subject is a negative, such as *nobody* or *nothing*.
> **Nobody** left any voice mail messages, **did they**?   Yes, they did. / No, they didn't.

1 Turn the statements into negative questions.

1. It would have been great if telemarketers had never gotten my number.
   Wouldn't it have been great if telemarketers had never gotten my number?
2. It was awful how much paper we wasted on fliers that nobody read.
3. Jill should have kept her text messages much shorter.
4. It was weird how those pop-up ads made my computer freeze.
5. It seemed like we spent all day looking for an Internet café.
6. It would have been great if we could have paid less for our computer.
7. We should have spent less time playing video games as kids.
8. It was sad how Mark got really addicted to social networking sites.

2 Complete the sentences with tag questions.

1. There were several voice mail messages for me, <u>weren't there</u>?
2. There haven't been any new rules about using social media at work, _____?
3. Someone told him there was a problem with his phone, _____?
4. You gave your computer password to someone, _____?
5. There was nothing he could do with his obsolete computer, _____?
6. Nobody we know ever actually clicked on those banner ads, _____?
7. She had already complained about the telemarketers, _____?
8. You used to have a robot vacuum that constantly cleaned the house, _____?

8A Reduced relative clauses

> **Non-defining relative clauses with *be* can be reduced in the same way as defining relative clauses. Notice the use of commas.**
> Einstein, **who is thought to be one of the greatest minds of the twentieth century,** struggled in school.
> Einstein, **thought to be one of the greatest minds of the twentieth century,** struggled in school.
> Curtis James Jackson III, **who is better known as the singer 50 Cent,** used to be a boxer.
> Curtis James Jackson III, **better known as the singer 50 Cent,** used to be a boxer.

1 Rewrite these sentences using reduced relative clauses.

1. The photographer who lives upstairs has won many awards for his creativity.
   The photographer living upstairs has won many awards for his creativity.

2. Professional cooking, which is considered a tough business, requires both patience and skill.

3. Movie stars who are constantly hounded by the press deserve more privacy.

4. Roger Federer, who is ranked among the world's best tennis players, is considered very disciplined.

5. The Summer Olympics, which are held every four years, are broadcast around the world.

6. Children who are talented at music should take private lessons if possible.

2 Combine the sentences. Rewrite them as one sentence containing a reduced non-defining relative clause.

1. Lady Gaga is generally believed to be very confident and professional. She claims she is actually shy.
   Lady Gaga, generally believed to be very confident and professional, claims she is actually shy.

2. Yohji Yamamoto is famous for his modern fashion designs. He often uses the color black.

3. Jessica Alba has been interested in acting since the age of five. She first appeared in a film at age 13.

4. The movie *Twilight* was adapted from a novel by Stephenie Meyer. It stars Robert Pattinson.

5. Mark Zuckerberg is celebrated for creating Facebook. He attended Harvard University.

6. Justin Bieber is originally from Canada. He began his professional singing career in the U.S.

7. Tim Berners-Lee is credited with inventing the Web. He published the first website in 1991.

8. Jamie Oliver is known for his food-focused TV shows. He advocates healthier food in schools.

8B Non-defining relative clauses as sentence modifiers

Non-defining relative clauses can be used as sentence modifiers and can contain almost any verb. Some of the most common ones are *surprise*, *depress*, *encourage*, *suggest (that)*, *contribute to*, and *result in*. Note that the verbs that describe emotion must be followed by an object.

My husband tried to repair a leak with aluminum foil, **which has resulted in a ruined silk carpet**.
My teacher praised my English today, **which encourages me to study harder**.
Peter has been happier since he took up golf, **which suggests that hobbies are good for a person both mentally and physically**.
I learned how to clean jewelry with toothpaste, **which depressed me because it meant I had wasted a fortune on expensive cleaners**.
I've started making my own clothes, **which has contributed to financial savings and a full closet**!

1 Match these statements with the appropriate non-defining clauses.

1. I use dental floss to string beads for jewelry, __c__
2. My sister always loved school, ____
3. Robert moved to a small town, ____
4. I just had a big fight with Ana, ____
5. Paul is really good at solving problems, ____
6. Amy jogs every morning, ____
7. I've had a private tutor for the past few months, ____
8. The class I wanted to take is already full, ____

a. which surprised us since he loves cities.
b. which has contributed to weight loss and more energy.
c. which is why I have so much of it.
d. which is why people always go to him for help.
e. which has resulted in better grades for me.
f. which encouraged her to go into teaching.
g. which means I'll have to explore alternatives in the course schedule.
h. which depressed me because she's my best friend.

2 Complete the sentences with a phrase from the box.

| which resulted in | which suggested | which depressed |
| which encouraged | which means | which surprised |

1. I'm working late tonight, _____which means_____ I'll take a later train home.
2. My friend was in a local play, _____ me to try acting.
3. Our team lost the championship, _____ me and my friends.
4. Prices went down last year, _____ savings for many people.
5. Ted sent me a nice birthday card, _____ me since he usually doesn't do anything special for people's birthdays.
6. Dinner tasted terrible, _____ that I didn't follow the recipe correctly.

9A Clauses and phrases showing contrast and exception

> The following are additional common phrases that show contrast and exception.
>
> Use *whereas*, especially in formal writing, to present contrasting information.
> **Whereas** the bottled water market is huge in Italy, it is very small in Japan.
>
> Use *except (for)* or *with the exception of* to show an exception within a group.
> Everyone in my family, **except for** my mother, plays a musical instrument.
> Everyone in my family, **with the exception of** my mother, plays a musical instrument.

1 Circle the correct answer to complete the sentence.

1. (While) / *Unlike* Leo prefers a big breakfast, I just have coffee.
2. No one in the class, *except that* / *with the exception of* Eva, can speak German.
3. *In contrast to* / *While* city people, those who live on farms must have a car.
4. *Unlike* / *Except for* Thai women, Spanish women greet each other with a kiss.
5. I'm a typical Canadian, *whereas* / *except for the fact that* I don't like hockey.
6. Most Americans have dinner by 7:00, *whereas* / *unlike* in Spain people eat later.
7. Everyone on our street, *except that* / *except for* my family, has a pet.
8. *Unlike* / *While* me, all my friends are addicted to reality shows on TV.

2 Read about Alonzo and Jun. Complete the sentences with an expression to show contrast or exception. More than one answer is possible.

Alonzo (26 years old) . . .	Jun (21 years old) . . .
finished college four years ago.	is in his third year of college.
considers himself to be pretty typical.	doesn't think he's really typical.
plays and watches all kinds of sports.	doesn't play any sports.
isn't crazy about baseball.	doesn't watch any sport but baseball.
has a high salary and eats out often.	doesn't work and always cooks at home.
wears a suit on weekdays.	always dresses very casually.

1. Jun is still in college, *whereas / while* Alonzo has already graduated.
2. Alonzo considers himself to be pretty typical, _____ Jun doesn't.
3. _____ Jun, Alonzo is a big sports fan.
4. Alonzo is a fan of most sports _____ baseball.
5. Alonzo has dinner in restaurants, _____ Jun usually can't afford to eat out.
6. _____ Alonzo, Jun hardly ever dresses up.
7. Alonzo has a good job, _____ Jun isn't working now.
8. Jun and Alonzo are very different, _____ they are both in their 20s.

9B Past habitual with *used to* and *would*

> To ask questions about a habitual action or situation in the past, use *Did . . . use to . . . ?* (NOT *Would . . . ?*).
> **Did you use to listen** to rock music when you were younger?
> **Did you use to share** a bedroom with your little brother?
>
> Use the negative question *Didn't . . . use to . . . ?* to confirm a guess about habitual actions or a situation in the past.
> **Didn't you use to work** at a grocery store after school?
> **Didn't he use to play** on the school soccer team?

1 Write the questions to these responses. Use *Did . . . use to* or *Didn't . . . use to*.

1. A: *Did / Didn't you use to live in San Francisco?*
   B: Yes, I did. I lived in San Francisco for about two years.

2. A: _____
   B: A lot? No, as a matter of fact, I've never drunk coffee.

3. A: _____
   B: No, he never did. Actually, Pete's allergic to cats.

4. A: _____
   B: In the school band? Yes, I did. I played the flute.

5. A: _____
   B: Yes, I always rode my bike in elementary school, but I'd take the bus on rainy days.

6. A: _____
   B: Yeah, my hair was really long, but I had to cut it when I joined the swim team.

2 Choose the correct answer to complete each sentence. Sometimes both are possible.

1. Lesley *would /* (*used to*) live in Brazil before she moved to Turkey.
2. We *would / used to* have fun during summer vacations.
3. They *would / used to* have a house by the ocean, but they've sold it.
4. Serena *would / used to* go mountain biking every weekend.
5. *Would her parents / Did her parents use to* own a Mexican restaurant ten years ago?
6. My mother *would / used to* volunteer at the hospital every winter.
7. Alex *would / used to* like to build models of cars and ships.
8. *Would you / Did you use to* be good at fixing cars when you were younger?

10A Relative clauses and noun clauses

> In some relative clauses, the relative pronoun (*who*, *that*, or *which*) can be omitted.
>
> In an object relative clause, a relative pronoun (*who*, *that*, or *which*) is optional. Relative pronouns are only required when they function as the subject of a relative clause.
> My friend told our classmates a secret. I had told him that secret.
> My friend told our classmates a secret (**that**) I had told him.
>
> In a subject relative clause, a relative pronoun (*who*, *that*, or *which*) is necessary because it functions as the subject of the relative clause.
> I have a roommate. She never cleans the kitchen.
> I have a roommate **who** never cleans the kitchen.

1 Choose the sentences where the relative pronoun (*who*, *that*, or *which*) is optional.

- ☑ 1. The restaurant that we had dinner at last night overcharged us.
- ☐ 2. One thing that makes me sick is really selfish people.
- ☐ 3. People who chew gum loudly really get on my nerves.
- ☐ 4. Someone's cell phone kept ringing all through the movie that I saw last night.
- ☐ 5. I had a big argument with a store clerk who refused to give me a refund.
- ☐ 6. My teacher gets mad at every little noise that our class makes.
- ☐ 7. The town fined a neighbor who burned garbage in her backyard.
- ☐ 8. The people in the line which he tried to cut into complained to the theater manager.

2 Complete the sentences with *who* or *that*. If the pronoun can be omitted, write *X*. Sometimes more than one answer is possible.

1. One thing ____*that*____ gets me down is people ___*who / that*___ lie to me.
2. I like people _____ stand up for something _____ they believe in.
3. Something _____ makes me sad is people _____ have no place to live.
4. Something _____ I can't do is keep up with technology.
5. I was a kid _____ had parents _____ made a lot of rules.
6. The thing _____ aggravates me most is people _____ are cruel to animals.

10B Simple and complex indirect questions

> **If the beginning clause of an indirect question is in statement word order, the sentence is a statement and ends with a period.**
> **I'm curious about** why he didn't complain to the landlord.
> **I'm not sure** who is responsible for repairing the roads.
> **The big question is** if / whether we can get the city officials to listen to our concerns.
>
> **If the beginning clause of an indirect question is in question word order, the sentence is a question and ends with a question mark.**
> **Do you have any idea** if / whether I need a visa to visit China?
> **Could you tell me** where I can go to pay my parking ticket?
> **Don't you wonder** how a place with such poor service stays in business?

1 Rewrite these sentences using the words in parentheses.

1. Why can't the city add more streetlights? (I don't understand . . .)
   I don't understand why the city can't add more streetlights.

2. Is the city going to improve the rush hour bus service? (Do you know . . .)

3. Why are prices going up so fast? (. . . is something that baffles me.)

4. How can I finish the work before the deadline? (I have no idea . . .)

5. Have you saved enough money for school? (Would you mind telling me . . .)

6. Why aren't there any bike paths in the city? (. . . is beyond me.)

7. How am I going to find time to enjoy myself? (My main problem is . . .)

8. When are they going to build a new hospital? (Do you have any idea . . .)

9. Who decided to close the swimming pool in the park? (Don't you wonder . . .)

10. Is tuition going up again next year? (I have to find out . . .)

2 Rewrite these sentences as direct questions.

1. I haven't got a clue what we're supposed to do for homework tonight.
   What are we supposed to do for homework tonight?

2. How people can leave their children home alone is mystifying to me.

3. What I don't get is how I can keep up with all this new technology.

4. Why there isn't a pedestrian zone downtown is my number-one question.

5. I'd like to know who should be responsible for keeping our city clean.

6. Tell me what I have to do to get my driver's license.

7. When the next meeting will be is something I haven't found out yet.

8. I wonder if I should complain about my neighbor's loud parties.

11A Present unreal conditional with *unless*, *only if*, and *even if*

> To ask a follow-up question after a yes/no question, a shortened conditional can be used, especially in spoken or informal English. The positive shortened conditional is *if so*, and the negative shortened conditional is *if not*.
> Would you consider lying to a good friend to avoid hurting your friend's feelings? **If so**, what kinds of things would you lie about?
> Are you sure your friends are loyal and trusting? **If not**, you shouldn't tell them your secrets.

1 Match the yes/no questions on the left with the follow-up questions on the right.

1. Would you say anything if a colleague called you by the wrong name? _c_
2. If the man next to you on the bus fell asleep on your shoulder, would you wake him up? ___
3. Would you remain silent if you disagreed with your boss in a meeting? ___
4. Would you report it if you saw a friend steal a small item from a store? ___
5. If people you secretly disliked invited you to a party at their home, would you go? ___
6. If a cat always came to your house for food, would you keep it? ___

a. If not, what would you say?
b. If not, would you confront your friend?
c. If so, what would you say?
d. If not, would you try to find its owner?
e. If so, how would you wake him up?
f. If not, what excuse would you give?

2 Review the rules for the present unreal conditional with *unless*, *only if*, and *even if* on page 89. Choose the correct answer to complete each sentence.

1. I wouldn't lie to a friend (*unless*) / *only if* it was in his or her best interests.
2. If you found money on the street, would you turn it in to the police?
   If so / *If not*, what would you do with it?
3. Would you report a shoplifter *only if* / *even if* the person looked poor?
   If so / *If not*, would you tell the store manager, or would you call the police?
4. He wouldn't lose his temper *only if* / *even if* he were really angry.
5. Would you confront a friend who gossiped about you behind your back?
   If so / *If not*, what would you say?
6. I wouldn't read anyone else's mail *even if* / *only if* I were really curious.
7. Would you make a promise if you already knew you couldn't keep it?
   If so / *If not*, what would you do later when you didn't keep the promise?
8. I would criticize my friends *unless* / *only if* I knew a way to help them improve.

11B Wishes and regrets

> Wishes and regrets often use comparative words, such as *(not) enough*, *more*, *less*, and *better*, and intensifiers, such as *really* and *very*.
>
> I did**n't** save **enough** money last summer.
> I wish I had saved **more** money last summer.
>
> I spent **too much** money on video games last year.
> If only I had spent **less** money on video games last year.
>
> I bought **too many** clothes this weekend.
> I wish I had bought **fewer** clothes this weekend.
>
> I do**n't** understand math very **well**.
> I wish I understood math **better**.
>
> I got **really** angry at my friend last night.
> If only I had**n't** gotten **so** angry at my friend last night.

1 Complete the wishes and regrets with a word from the box.

| better | fewer | harder | less | more | so |

1. I don't have enough time to do volunteer work.
   I wish I had ____*more*____ time to do volunteer work.

2. I don't know how to swim very well.
   I wish I knew how to swim _____.

3. I drank too much coffee before bed last night.
   If only I had drunk _____ coffee before bed last night.

4. The teacher thought the questions on the exam were much too easy.
   The teacher wished the questions on the exam had been _____.

5. Our class has too many assignments this week.
   I wish our class had _____ assignments this week.

6. I felt really sleepy in class and couldn't pay any attention.
   I wish I hadn't felt _____ sleepy in class and had paid attention.

2 Rewrite these sentences using the words in parentheses.

1. I wasn't very obedient in elementary school. (I wish . . .)
   I wish I had been more obedient in elementary school.

2. I refused to take piano lessons when I was young. (If only . . .)

3. I fell asleep at the computer last night, and now my essay is late. (I wish . . . Then . . .)

4. I exercised too much yesterday, so now I feel really tired. (If only . . . Then . . .)

5. Bob is shy and doesn't make friends easily. (Bob wishes . . .)

6. I'm not a very good cook. (If only . . .)

12A Future perfect and future perfect continuous

> When using the future perfect or future perfect continuous, the particular point in the future is often referred to in another part of the sentence.
> **By this time next year**, your commitment to language study is going to have gotten stronger.
> **On August 1**, I will have been living overseas for six months.
> **After a few months**, you're going to have made real progress with English.
> **Before next spring**, he will have finished most of his course work.
> **By the time you arrive in New York**, Marisa will have already received the package you sent.
> **When the van arrives**, I will have been packing for two days, and I probably won't have finished.
> **Before I leave for Paris**, I will already have sold my house and put my things in storage.
> **After I finish this**, I will have completed everything on my "to do" list.

1 Underline the words in each sentence that refer to a point in the future.

1. <u>By the spring</u>, Nate will have visited over a dozen different countries.
2. When the end of the week arrives, I will have written four exams.
3. Before long, I'll have been working on this puzzle for an hour. It's impossible!
4. I can't believe he's still sleeping! At 11:00, he'll have been sleeping for 12 hours.
5. When she leaves the house, she'll have had six cups of coffee.
6. If it continues, on Tuesday it will have been raining for three weeks.
7. After I stop working, I will have painted three of the rooms in my house.
8. By the time the plane lands, we will have been in the air for seven hours.

2 Complete the sentences with the future perfect or the future perfect continuous form of the verb in parentheses.

1. By the end of class, I __*will have learned*__ (learn) about the future perfect tense.
2. By the year 2030, I _____ (work) for several years.
3. Before she's 30, Sue _____ (make) her first million dollars.
4. At the end of his trip, Seth _____ (visit) four different countries.
5. After I finish this book, I _____ (read) all the titles you recommended.
6. By 11:00, how long _____ Dan _____ (watch) TV?
7. When I finish college, I _____ (be) in school for 16 years.
8. Pretty soon, I _____ (wait) for her for an hour. I'm getting annoyed!
9. We're late. By the time we get there, they _____ (finish) dinner.
10. On Friday of this week, Kara _____ (travel) for two months.

12B Mixed conditionals

Conditionals can appear in many forms. They can describe how situations in the past affect situations in the past, the present, or the future.

Use a past form in both the *if* clause and the result clause to talk about true events in the past.
When I was younger, if I **didn't behave** well, my parents **were** disappointed.
If we **got** lost during our trip last year, we just **asked** someone for directions.

Use the past perfect in the *if* clause and *would / wouldn't have* + the past participle of the verb in the result clause to talk about hypothetical situations in the past that had effects on the more recent past.
If I **had been born** with a good voice, I **would have started** my own band a long time ago.

Use the past perfect in the *if* clause and *would / wouldn't* + verb in the result clause to describe hypothetical situations in the past that have effects on the present.
If I **had studied** harder when I was in school, I **would have** a better job today.

Use the past perfect in the *if* clause and *would / wouldn't* + verb in the result clause to talk about hypothetical situations in the past that have effects on the future.
If she **had booked** her flight before now, she **would be** in Paris next week.
If I **hadn't taken** a year off from school, I **would be graduating** this June.

Complete these sentences with the correct form of the verbs in parentheses. Sometimes more than one answer is possible.

1. As a kid, I always ___enjoyed___ (enjoy) school if I _____ (like) the teacher.
2. If I _____ (study) harder last year, I _____ (not have to) repeat the course this year.
3. If he _____ (not speak) Greek, his trip to Athens last year _____ (be) so enjoyable.
4. When I was young, if I _____ (see) a scary movie, I _____ (have) bad dreams.
5. When I was a kid, if my father _____ (go away) on a business trip, he always _____ (call) at 8:00 to say "Good night" to us.
6. If I _____ (spend) less money when I was younger, I _____ (have) a nice little nest egg in a few years.
7. If I _____ (not have) a fight with my friend yesterday, I _____ (go) to the party tonight.
8. If she _____ (show) more interest since she was hired, she _____ (get) the next promotion.
9. If I _____ (not lose) my passport, I _____ (fly) to Lisbon tonight.
10. If she _____ (not start) figure skating when she was four, she _____ (not be) in the last Olympics.

VOCABULARY PLUS

7A Technology buzzwords

Use four words from the box to correct the underlined mistakes in the sentences.

| apps | the cloud | download | post | spyware | Wi-Fi |

1. My aunt recently started to <u>text</u> her recipes online to share with others. _____
2. Kyle said that <u>a blog</u> was secretly recording my online activity. _____
3. Angela downloaded some <u>podcasts</u> to play games on her smartphone. _____
4. My apartment building has installed <u>a virus</u>, so I can use my laptop anywhere in the building to get on the Internet. _____

7A Expressions for connecting ideas formally

Choose the correct words to complete the text.

Does technology keep you up at night?

Technology has had a positive impact on our lives, for the most part. (1) *Similarly / (As a matter of fact) / Additionally*, it's hard to imagine how we could live without our computers, smartphones, and apps. These things have made our lives so easy! (2) *Therefore / Nevertheless / As a result*, some technology issues keep me up at night. (3) *Likewise / On the other hand / For example*, what can we do about spyware? As soon as we download software to get rid of it, someone creates a new way to spy on our computers. (4) *For instance / In fact / Furthermore*, there's spyware's nasty cousin, the virus, which can ruin anyone's day. It's a constant battle to overcome these issues, but we can take some common sense steps. Always remember to back up your documents. (5) *In fact / Additionally / As a result*, update your software whenever you get alerts from the manufacturers. Doing these things can help keep technology a positive part of daily life.

7B Words for forms of communication

Cross out the words that do <u>not</u> fit the meaning of the sentences.

A: We're planning an ad campaign to launch a new athletic shoe. In addition to some television ads that look like cool music videos, we'll use (1) *billboards / ~~voice mail~~ / bumper stickers*.

B: Are you also considering (2) *banner ads / pop-up ads / spam* to reach wider audiences?

A: Yes, they're on our list of possibilities. We're also wondering if we should hire a professional basketball player to appear on (3) *a crawl / a bus wrap / an infomercial*.

B: That's a great idea. Now, you may want to know that our research showed that younger audiences think print ads are old-fashioned. They want everything to be digital, so don't use (4) *fliers / billboards / pop-up ads* anymore.

8A Qualities of creative people

Match the correct words to complete the sentences.

1. Nora has the ___f___ to practice daily to achieve her dream of becoming an opera singer.
2. The director was _____ when he chose the actors for the cast. He chose quickly, and didn't ask anyone back for a second audition.
3. Ellie has been on several archeological digs in Asia and is _____ about ancient Chinese and Korean cultures.
4. Pablo is _____ to complete five paintings to enter in the art competition this spring.
5. Gino is _____ in his business; for example, he uses recycled materials to build homes.
6. Chad's science fiction stories are set 500 years in the future and show great _____.

a. decisive
b. resourceful
c. determined
d. knowledgeable
e. originality
f. discipline

8B Collocations for problem solving

Choose the correct words to complete the text.

Groupware

If you ever worked for a multinational company in the past, you know that sometimes it could take hours just to set up a meeting with your colleagues. To help improve productivity, technology companies explored various ways to (1) *find a mistake /* (*find a solution*) to the problem. They studied the way people worked and (2) *made a mistake / analyzed this information* to figure out how companies might work together more effectively and efficiently. Technological innovators (3) *explored the possibilities of / found problems for* using networked computers and digital office tools. Eventually, they were able to (4) *solve this problem / analyze the problem* by designing groupware, which is software that helps groups of people work together and share information on the Internet. With groupware, colleagues can set up a meeting quickly and have meetings via video, across several continents. And electronic file-sharing systems allow workers to (5) *find alternatives / organize information* and share documents instantly. Problem solved!

9A Expressions related to accepting or changing things

Choose the correct words to complete the conversation.

Amber: I just met your sister. She's so passionate about changing society! She really wants to (1) *follow the crowd* / *make waves* / *fit in*.

Becca: Oh yes, Olivia and I are pretty different. I tend to follow the rules and am much more (2) *conventional* / *rebellious* / *unconventional* than she is.

Amber: What was it like growing up in your family? Did your parents teach you to behave yourself and (3) *accept* / *stand up to* / *confront* society's rules?

Becca: Actually, our parents were pretty (4) *unconventional* / *amenable* / *conservative* in their attitudes. At a time when most of their friends were becoming bankers and lawyers, my parents helped set up food pantries to feed poor people in our town.

Amber: Well, that helps explain why Olivia is so active in organizing that free tutoring program at the community center. But why do you think you're so different from her?

Becca: I guess it's just my personality. I want to help people, but I'm kind of shy and don't like to (5) *fit in* / *follow the crowd* / *confront* people.

Amber: I think that's good! You're (6) *being your own person* / *being rebellious* / *making waves* after all.

9B Expressions with *keep* and *stay*

Replace the underlined words in each sentence with an expression from the box above that means the same thing.

| keep in touch | keep out of trouble | keep things in perspective | stay awake |

1. Sofia is moving to a new neighborhood, but her friends hope she will <u>stay connected</u>.

   Sofia is moving to a new neighborhood, but her friends hope she will ___*keep in touch*___.

2. When Pedro gets stressed out about his challenging new job, he tries to <u>remember what's truly important in life</u>.

   When Pedro gets stressed out about his challenging new job, he tries to _____.

| keep connected | keep up with | stay awake | stay out of trouble |

3. Our economics class is difficult, and the professor assigns so many reports and research projects. How do you <u>get it all done</u>?

   How do you _____ it all?

4. Ever since Jack changed schools, he's been hanging out with the wrong crowd. I hope he can <u>avoid getting into a bad situation</u>.

   I hope he can _____.

10A Expressions with *drive*, *get*, and *make*

Cross out the words that do not fit the meaning of the sentences.

Hey, friends, I just returned from a wonderful trip to Bangkok! What amazing street life there! And the food was so spicy and delicious. But traveling there drove (1) *me crazy / me down / me mad*. My flight from Los Angeles was cancelled because of some bad storms. There were long lines to rebook flights, but what made (2) *my blood boil / me mad / on my nerves* was the airline's terrible customer service. It took an hour to get my ticket for a new flight, and then I had to wait two more hours to get through security. Standing in line always gets (3) *me sick / on my nerves / under my skin*. I got stuck behind a family with six noisy, spoiled kids. I was thinking to myself, "Excuse me, but I just used all of my savings for this ticket, and I have to board my flight in 10 minutes!" Talk about driving (4) *someone upset / someone up a wall / someone mad!*

When I finally got on the plane, I ended up sitting next to a guy who kept talking about his big, important job. He bragged so much that it made (5) *my blood boil / me down / me mad*. To get him to stop talking, I pretended to fall asleep. I was so happy when our flight landed!

10B *-ed* words that describe feelings

Use words from each box to correct the underlined mistakes in the sentences.

baffled   infuriated   insulted

1. Max read over the instructions in his new computer manual several times, but he was still <u>stunned</u>. The instructions were not written very clearly. _____**baffled**_____

2. My boss is impatient and gets angry when she has to wait for things. She was <u>saddened</u> that she had to wait for six months to get a refund for a defective cell phone. _____

3. In some cultures, people feel <u>enraged</u> if new acquaintances refuse to shake hands. _____

frustrated   mystified   stunned

4. Julia was <u>confused</u> because her rent was due on the first of the month, but she wouldn't get her paycheck until the following week. _____

5. After the doctor disappeared, the detective conducted a thorough investigation. Even after analyzing all the evidence, he was still <u>demoralized</u> about what had actually happened. _____

6. Vicky didn't think her violin audition went very well, so she was <u>humiliated</u> to learn that the conductor had selected her for first chair in the orchestra. _____

11A Forming antonyms with prefixes

Choose the true statement for each sentence.

1. Nick thinks it's unethical to tell a white lie, even if it's to protect someone's feelings.
   - ☑ a. Nick thinks it's dishonest to tell a white lie.
   - ☐ b. Nick thinks it's irresponsible to tell a white lie.

2. Mai believes that making wishes is irrational, and that it gives people false hopes.
   - ☐ a. Mai thinks that making wishes is disagreeable.
   - ☐ b. Mai thinks that making wishes is illogical.

3. The accountant is scrupulous about tracking all of the company's profits.
   - ☐ a. The accountant is agreeable.
   - ☐ b. The accountant is responsible.

4. Most lawyers think the judge has a solid reputation for being trustworthy.
   - ☐ a. The judge's behavior is ethical.
   - ☐ b. The judge's behavior is unacceptable.

5. The investigator reported that the bank's lending practices may be unscrupulous.
   - ☐ a. The bank's lending practices may be illegal.
   - ☐ b. The bank's lending practices may be irrational.

6. It's unfair to copy test answers from another student.
   - ☐ a. It's illogical to copy test answers from another student.
   - ☐ b. It's unethical to copy test answers from another student.

11B Adjectives and nouns referring to personal values

Choose the correct words to complete the conversation.

Yoko: One quality I value in my friends is (1) *indifference / selfishness /* (compassion).

Omar: I agree! I also think it's important for friends to be (2) *honest / tender / generous* if they think I'm doing something wrong.

Yoko: It's helpful when my friends are truthful, but I also want them to be (3) *selfish / sensitive / resilient*. I don't want them to hurt my feelings.

Omar: Yeah, I guess that's important. You know, I wish some of my friends were better at keeping secrets! They need to show a little (4) *discretion / kindness / tolerance* when I share something personal.

Yoko: That's true! I expect my friends to have (5) *generosity / resilience / respect* for my privacy. I'm pretty open, but it's annoying when people ask too many questions.

Omar: Yeah, some people are too curious. But, I think overall, my friends are (6) *kind and generous / sensitive and selfish / resilient and indifferent*, and they make me happy!

12A Expressions ending with prepositions

Choose the correct words to complete the email.

Hi Jill,

I heard that you're moving to Tokyo soon to teach English. That's something to (1) *be scared of* / *(be excited about)*!

I remember that when I moved to Buenos Aires last year, it took a while to (2) *get accustomed to* / *look forward to* a new culture. I had to learn about the way people do business, make friends, and have fun. Luckily, I can speak Spanish, so I was able to (3) *be familiar with* / *participate in* meetings and conversations. I wanted to (4) *take advantage of* / *become aware of* cultural events, so I attended concerts, saw plays, and even learned to play guitar from an Argentinean musician!

My advice is to keep an open mind and give yourself time to (5) *adjust to* / *take advantage of* your new home. And don't (6) *be scared of* / *become aware of* trying new things.

I (7) *am familiar with* / *look forward to* hearing about your adventures in Japan!

Henry

12B Compound adjectives

Combine words from the boxes to make compound adjectives to complete the travel tips. Some words will be used more than once. Sometimes more than one answer is possible.

| culturally | non | open | self |

| assured | aware | judgmental | minded | reliant | sensitive |

Travel Tips

1. Be ___**open-minded**___ about trying new kinds of food. You may be captivated by a new cuisine!

2. Be _____ when it comes to exploring places on your own. You want people to think you're a confident, experienced traveler.

3. Be _____ when you experience new cultures. Consider all sides of an issue before forming an opinion.

4. People tolerate different levels of risk. Be _____ and assess your own tolerance for adventure, uncertainty, and possible danger when you plan your trips.

5. If you're traveling on business, learn about local customs and manners and try to be _____ when you meet with clients.

6. If you're going to hike in the mountains, prepare to be _____. Pack essentials such as water, food, rope, maps, a flashlight, and a first-aid kit.

Credits

Illustration credits

Charlene Chua: 8
Jo Goodberry: 20, 40, 60, 86
Brad Hamann: 72
Paul Hostetler: 5, 32, 33, 49, 51, 61, 78
Kim Johnson: 17, 43, 70, 80, 81
Larry Jost: 48
Dan McGeehan: 12, 55, 76, 93
Rob Schuster: 27, 28, 57
Koren Shadmi: 36, 88, 97, 133
James Yamasaki: 42, 82, 90, 104

Photography credits

Back cover: (*clockwise from top center*) ©Leszek Bogdewicz/Shutterstock, ©Wavebreak Media/Thinkstock, ©Blend Images/Alamy, ©limpido/Shutterstock; **2** ©iStock Collection/Thinkstock; **3** (*left to right*) ©iStock Collection/Thinkstock, ©Blend Images/Thinkstock, ©Stockbyte/Thinkstock, ©Digital Vision/Thinkstock; **4** (*top to bottom*) ©Purestock/SuperStock, ©iStock Collection/Thinkstock; **6** (*left to right*) ©Exactostock/SuperStock, ©yu liang wong/Alamy, ©Inmagine/Alamy; **7** ©Monkey Business/Thinkstock; **9** ©Stockbyte/Thinkstock; **10** (*left to right*) ©iStock Collection/Thinkstock, ©iStock Collection/Thinkstock, ©PhotoObjects/Thinkstock; **11** ©I love images/men's lifestyle/Alamy; **13** ©iStock Collection/Thinkstock; **14** (*top to bottom*) ©Gary Lee/Photoshot/Newscom, ©Courtesy of Banksy, ©Lia/Listal, ©Kathy deWitt/Alamy; **15** (*clockwise from top left*) ©Jupiterimages/Thinkstock, ©iStock Collection/Thinkstock, ©PHOTOPQR/L'ALSACE/Newscom; **16** ©NHPA/SuperStock; **18** (*clockwise from top left*) ©eye35.pix/Alamy, ©MIVA Stock/SuperStock, ©JTB PHOTO COMMUNICATI/JTB Photo/SuperStock, ©imagebroker.net/SuperStock; **19** ©Medioimages/Photodisc/Thinkstock; **21** (*top to bottom*) ©Neale Cousland/Shutterstock, ©iStock Collection/Thinkstock; **22** (*left to right*) ©John Foxx/Thinkstock, ©Brian Jannsen/Alamy; **24** (*clockwise from top left*) ©iStock Collection/Thinkstock, ©Jupiterimages/Thinkstock, ©Robert_s/Shutterstock; **25** (*top to bottom*) ©iStock Collection/Thinkstock, ©Hemis.fr/SuperStock; **26** ©Jupiterimages/Thinkstock; **27** (*top to bottom*) ©Blend Images/SuperStock, ©Prisma/SuperStock; **28** (*left to right*) ©Wavebreak Media/Thinkstock, ©iStock Collection/Thinkstock, ©iStock Collection/Thinkstock, ©Comstock/Thinkstock; **29** ©iStock Collection/Thinkstock; **30** ©Wavebreak Media/Thinkstock; **31** ©iStock Collection/Thinkstock; **35** ©iStock Collection/Thinkstock; **37** ©PhotoAlto/SuperStock; **38** (*left to right*) ©Tetra Images/SuperStock, ©Fancy Collection/SuperStock; **39** ©Ryouchin/Getty Images; **40** (*left to right*) ©Comstock/Thinkstock, ©Andrea Morini/Thinkstock, ©iStock Collection/Thinkstock; **44** ©Alain SHRODER/Getty Images; **45** ©iStock Collection/Thinkstock; **46** ©Ammit/Thinkstock; **47** ©Greg Wahl-Stephens/Associated Press; **50** ©Purestock/Thinkstock; **52** ©iStock Collection/Thinkstock; **53** ©Jupiterimages/Thinkstock; **54** ©iStock Collection/Thinkstock; **56** ©iStock Collection/Thinkstock; **58** (*clockwise from top left*) ©Jupiterimages/Thinkstock, ©Creates Images/Thinkstock, ©iStock Collection/Thinkstock, ©Blend Images/SuperStock; **62** (*left to right*) ©iStock Collection/Thinkstock, ©Karen Moskowitz/Getty Images, ©Mircea Bezergheanu/Shutterstock, ©Comstock/Thinkstock; **03** ©Zuma Press, Inc/Alamy; **65** ©iStock Collection/Thinkstock; **66** (*left to right*) ©Ablestock Collection/Thinkstock, ©iStock Collection/Thinkstock, ©You Touch Pix of EuToch/Shutterstock; **67** (*left to right*) ©iStock Collection/Thinkstock, ©Fuse Collection/Thinkstock, ©iStock Collection/Thinkstock; **68** (*left to right*) ©Bloomberg/Getty Images, ©Denise Kappa/Shutterstock; **69** ©Yoshikazu Tsuno/AFP/Getty Images/Newscom; **73** ©meshaphoto/Getty Images; **74** ©Kinga/Shutterstock; **75** (*left to right*) ©Glow Images/Getty Images, ©iStock Collection/Thinkstock, ©Image Source/Thinkstock; **77** (*left to right*) ©prudkov/Shutterstock, ©prudkov/Shutterstock; **79** ©Wavebreak Media/Thinkstock; **84** (*clockwise from top left*) ©Allison Joyce/Stringer/Getty Images, ©iStock Collection/Thinkstock, ©iStock Collection/Thinkstock, ©Stockbyte/Thinkstock, ©GoGo Images Corporations/Alamy, ©mikute/Shutterstock; **87** ©Andrew Vaughan/Associated Press; **91** ©Wavebreak Media/Thinkstock; **92** (*top to bottom*) ©iStock Collection/Thinkstock, ©Jupiterimages/Thinkstock, ©Hemera Collection/Thinkstock, ©Digital Vision/Thinkstock, ©Exactostock/SuperStock, ©iStock Collection/Thinkstock; **94** ©RubberBall/Alamy; **95** ©NY Daily News/Getty Images; **98** (*top to bottom*) ©Harry How/Staff/Getty Images, ©Robin Smith/Getty Images; **100** ©Design Pics/SuperStock; **101** (*left to right*) ©Belinda Images/SuperStock, ©frans lemmens/Alamy, ©I love images/city break/Alamy; **102** (*left to right*) ©iStock Collection/Thinkstock, ©Top Photo Group/Thinkstock, ©iStock Collection/Thinkstock; **103** ©Morgan David de Lossy/Corbis; **130** ©AFP/Getty Images; **135** ©Aurora Photos/Alamy; **137** ©Cultura Creative/Alamy; **141** ©Michael Coyne/Getty Images

Text credits

The authors and publishers acknowledge the following sources of copyright material and are grateful for the permissions granted. While every effort has been made, it has not always been possible to identify the sources of all the material used, or to trace all copyright holders. If any omissions are brought to our notice, we will be happy to include the appropriate acknowledgments on reprinting.

9 Adapted from "My Tribe," by Erin Peterson, *Experience Life*, September 2005. Reproduced with permission of Erin Peterson; **17** Adapted from "Amnesia Spoils Newlyweds' Bliss," *ABC News*, June 30, 2005. Reproduced with permission of ABC News; **43** Adapted from "What Type of Cell Phone User Are You?" by Nancy Friedman. Reprinted with permission of Telephone Doctor Customer Service Training in St. Louis, MO. Nancy Friedman, President, is a keynote speaker at association meetings and Chamber of Commerce events as well as corporate gatherings. Call 314.291.1012 for more information or visit the website at www.telephonedoctor.com; **61** Adapted from "Brother, can you spare a dime for my Gucci bills?" by Janelle Brown, *Salon*, October 2, 2002. This article first appeared in Salon.com, at www.salon.com. An online version remains in the Salon archives. Reprinted with permission; **69** Adapted from "Mr. Song and Dance Man," by Dr. David McNeill, *Japan Focus*. Reproduced with permission of Dr. David McNeill, Sophia University, Tokyo; **77** Adapted from "4 Ways to Brush Up Your Problem-Solving Skills," by Barbara T. Armstrong, October 24, 2012. Reproduced with permission of Barbara T. Armstrong, Kahler Slater, Inc.; **87** Adapted from "Dave Carroll is still having problems with airlines," by Ellen Roseman, *The Toronto Star*, May 18, 2012. Reprinted with permission of Torstar Syndication Services; **103** Adapted from "Get Yourself Lost," by Arthur Frommer, *Travel Holiday*, September 1994.

Answers

Page 44, Exercise 1B: Story 3 is false.